Double My Revenues In 12 Months Or Less

A Guide to Consistent Business Growth Through Developing Profitable Systems And Automated Marketing

Cover Art by Dennis Morales Francis

Double My Revenues In 12 Months Or Less

Did Publishing, Inc.

10400 Twin Cities Road, Ste. 20 #113

Phone: (209) 200-9562

Fax: (209) 744-4331

Email: support@didpublishing.com

http://www.didpublishing.com

Web: www.evenbetterseo.com

Copyright © 2008 DiD Publishing, Inc.

ISBN 978-0-9764181-1-5

Table of Contents

Dedication

This book is dedicated to my family; to my mother, Grethel Francis, my wife, Tiffani, as well as my sons, Jordan and Dyson for patiently waiting while I'm forever busy creating my dream projects. They keep me well loved, well-grounded and constantly entertained.

Acknowledgments

I wish to thank several people who were instrumental in my marketing education. These folks can be found on the Internet and I feel would be of great benefit to your education as well. They will be showing up from time to time on the DMR Core Training schedule in the coming months.

My sincere thanks to:

Ben Hart

Chet Holmes

Christina Hills

Dan Kennedy

Jill Lublin

Jim Edwards

Mark Joyner

Robert Hartung

Ryan Deiss

Seth Godin

Double My Revenues In 12 Months Or Less

The 5 Dangerous Business Trends

Small businesses employ more than half of the private sector work force, produce more than half of private sector output, fill niche markets, innovate, and contribute to the competition in free markets.

Small businesses are overrepresented in business turnover; that is, they have relatively high rates of company startups and closures. The life span of the average small business is still three to five years.

Small businesses give individuals the chance to achieve their own versions of the American Dream, and allow entry into employment by individuals and demographic groups who might otherwise be shut out of the labor market.

Small businesses pay a disproportionate amount of the taxes while receiving less than equitable support than larger businesses.

Let's take a look at the 5 most dangerous business trends to avoid. We'll keep you from making the fatal business mistakes that causes others to fail. If you find that you're currently making some of these errors, admit it, make a note of it and get ready to fix it.

The reason that we are covering the mistakes of business first is to get you to understand that you must clean your house before you replace the furniture. It makes sense to avoid the usual pitfalls before working on doubling your income. Because the biggest challenge to small businesses today is incompetence.

Hard on the heels of Incompetence (46%) is Unbalanced Experience (30%), Complacency (12%) followed by Lack of Experience (11%) in the specified field of business, and finally, Neglect, Fraud, or Disaster. These are the leading causes of failure in business today.

These five opponents to your profit margin must be carefully monitored if you want to do more than just make a living with your business.

Let's start with incompetence. We aren't saying that people who start businesses are dumb. We mean that they usually start with very little competence in business affairs. They might be experts in their field but not in the complexity of running a business.

The proof of that statement is that 46% of all business failures are caused by a basic misunderstanding about what it takes to run a business.

Take a look at this list and burn it in your memory. These are the leading causes of failure in businesses today. Notice that being stupid is not on that list.

The good news is that incompetence can be beaten out of you with knowledge and experience. (Silently read list.)

The second major cause of failure is unbalanced experience. If you just got out of dental school and are extremely talented in your craft, that's great but if you don't have a head for business, then you may not be ready to take on that challenge at this time.

Let's look at a few of the causes of unbalanced experience.

These are usually caused by ad hoc business practices or inconsistent application of policies and procedures.

Complacency usually occurs during the mid-phase of the business cycle when owners and managers are doing well but not keeping up with current trends and competitive measures. They are simply coasting.

The entrepreneurial spirit is replaced with lethargy and mediocrity. Competition soon overtakes them and the marketplace makes them obsolete.

11% of the people who go into business do not know their market well enough to survive as a viable operation. There is that small minority of businesses that suffer from fraud and disaster; a mere 1%.

Taxes and Inflation

Another enemy of business is one that we rarely see coming. If you analyze your income and you're growing by less than 10% a year, you're going backward. Real inflation is usually higher than the government estimates. For obvious reasons; they have a vested interest in keeping the numbers slow. Your business has to live in the real world.

Along with inflation you'll also deal with the various taxes and fees that have to be paid. These don't seem to go down each year; just the opposite. They all take away from your bottom line.

The last word on taxes; do not rely on tax cuts to shore up your annual returns. If you are not profitable, you will not be able to take full advantage of tax breaks anyway.

Let's look at the odds for a moment. The NFIB estimations are grim at first glance. Remember that the majority of small business owners do not get an education in business before they open their doors.

That is why they wake up one day to realize that they are making little or no money regardless of how much they bring in.

The bigger you are the easier it is to succeed.

The fewer the employees, the greater your chances of failure! The facts lead to some interesting conclusions. Those businesses that can maintain a large staff tend to have systems in place to give direction and purpose to its employees. That in turn leads to greater income that does not rely on the business owner's direct input. The business owner is now free to grow the business instead of working in the business.

So you see that the main cause of business failure is redeemable. We can, through proper education and planning, take care of this problem. If you are in trouble financially, you should seek immediate financial counseling. You may be able to get help from your local SCORE program or the SBA.

In the next chapter we'll look at what successful companies are doing.

The wrap up:

If you take the time to study the mistakes of others, you will have a better chance of success.

Again, here are the top 5 reasons for business failure:

Incompetence (46%)

Unbalanced Experience (30%)

Complacency (12%)

Lack of Experience (11%)

Neglect, fraud, or Disaster (1%)

These are the leading causes of failure in business today.

Successful Solutions

What's the difference between a hugely successful company and one that's struggling year after year?

As more research keeps pointing out, successful business owners remain passionate about their purpose in the company. They're confident in the direction their companies are going.

Successful companies have four vital components working effectively without the need of the owners' direct day-to-day supervision.

They have systems in place to handle these vital areas. Those key components are...

Money, Management, Marketing and Operations

Let's look at the money.

It takes a while for start-ups to break even because unforeseen contingencies always develop. In the interim, owners still need to support their businesses and families. This is a crucial time.

Smart business owners plan for such contingencies by securing three times the amount of capital estimated for operations. This avoids the need to for premature second round of financing during the startup phase.

Three phases of business development cycle: Start-up, Operation and Expansion.

These three phases of business require different strategic financial plans in order to achieve the business's goals. It's important to recognize where your business fits in the business development cycle.

Management

The vast majority of aspiring entrepreneurs fill their management ranks with friends. This is not only the surest way to break up a friendship; it is also the most predictable way to achieve failure.

Successful business owners never hire acquaintances to join their management team unless they have management experience appropriate to the field of their business and they are willing to openly disagree with them.

You will need an outside management advisory team as well as outside consultants. These resources will fill in as advisors for your business. Essential advisors to your team will be legal, accounting and financial.

Let's look at marketing

Marketing must become a priority in order to consistently deliver maximum performance in acquiring revenue.

Marketing must create Top of Mind Awareness. This means that the people, who need your product or services most, should have YOU in mind when the need arises.

There are 7 indispensable components of effective marketing. The most successful businesses use most or all of these in a systematic and strategic plan.

They are:

1. Advertising

2. Public Relations

3. Direct Mail

4. Personal Sales

6. Internet

7. Print Promotions

Successful businesses are proactive in developing operational systems. Whether you provide a product or deliver a service, establishing policies and procedures helps you to succeed in the long run.

Which business would you buy; the one without an organized system for success or the one that consistently charted its growth and planned for success? How would you be able to quantify the value of the business that had no definite policies and procedures? How would you effectively duplicate that business?

If you want to establish successful systems, imagine that your business had over 100 locations and each location ran their operations at the peak of efficiency. What standards and practices can you establish now that will replicate in 100 locations?

You might be saddled with the constraints and limited flexibility of a franchise without the brand recognition and solid systems that a large company can provide.

Many entrepreneurs who find that they cannot adapt to the changing conditions of business fall by the wayside and the franchiser then pulls the license and sells it to someone else. Keep in mind that your company's marketing will always be up to you even if you own a franchise.

Important Note!

If you're having a rough time in business, and you have to make cuts, go without food before you cut your marketing. Find the areas of your marketing that's working and put your money there. Cut the money from areas that's not bringing in prospects, not bringing in buyers and not making you money. Many business owners cut marketing first because they haven't got a clue if it's working or not. They spend money on marketing with unrealistic expectations and then pull the investment before the results can be achieved.

Growing and maintaining a small business is not easy. It takes stamina, patience and perseverance to keep the doors open every day. It also takes money and marketing to succeed at getting your message to the right prospects. Small business owners need to pay close attention to the message they convey and how it is perceived by their target audience in order to their promotional budget.

Knowing what works and what doesn't in the arena of promotional advertising and marketing is one of the most common problems business owners face. When you are working with limited resources it is extremely difficult to apportion time and money to every new idea that comes around. This is one reason why Internet marketing has still eluded a lot of local companies. They often don't know what to do and where to best allocate resources.

Trying to keep up with the various trends that seem to pop up on a regular basis takes a lot of work and no small business owner has the time keep up when they must also wear 100 other hats in their industry. What I found is that the basic principles of marketing still holds true even in the digital age regardless of the type of product or service being offered there are still fundamental applications that fit even the most cutting-edge marketing model. I have distilled the processes down to a basic set of tools that any business owner can use to succeed at generating leads.

There are 18 marketing tools that are vital to the health and growth of a small business in today's competitive world. There is no doubt that technology has made life easier for small business operation but it is also made it more frustrating. But the essence of marketing is still finding and influencing the people who have a need for what you are selling. You can use any of these 18 tools in a variety of configurations based on your budget or unique requirements.

1. A Company Website
2. A Separate Blog
3. Affiliate Or Referral Program
4. Customer Retention Program
5. Direct Mail
6. E-Mail Marketing
7. Google Maps
8. Internet Advertising
9. Monthly Articles
10. Monthly Newsletters
11. Online Video Channel
12. Podcast Channel
13. Print Ads
14. Radio and Television Advertising
15. Regular Press Releases
16. Search Engine Marketing
17. Social Media Interaction
18. Telemarketing

These tools offer your business a fighting chance at staying ahead of the competition and can also dramatically improve your bottom line. I wouldn't necessarily stress one particular tool over another because they all have their pluses and minuses when it comes to effectiveness based on particular markets. It isn't necessary to utilize all the tools every month; that may be impractical for many small businesses.

If you are just starting to pay attention to marketing, choose a collection of tools that can easily be tracked to gauge their performance. For example establish a company website and a separate blog. Use e-mail marketing and direct mail to promote your company. Establish a customer retention program and affiliate or referral program using your e-mail marketing campaign and direct mail campaign to generate interest.

Craft your message and stick to it. Conduct market research and establish a series of keywords that can be used throughout your promotional campaign both on the web and off-line. Keep your message consistent with the keywords in order to generate a solid message to a target audience.

Promote your message through a variety of media sources for example articles and video or develop a podcast series dealing with the specific topics surrounding your message. Get the word out through social networks and your blog and drive traffic and search engine marketing techniques.

Sketch out your entire campaign on the calendar in order to simplify the entire process. This also allows you to identify your milestones and help in tracking your progress. Marketing should never be an afterthought in your business. Delivering your message and converting prospects to customers is essential for generating consistent profits.

The wrap up:

Systems will serve you well once you put them in place and test them for consistent effectiveness. Remember that systems allow you to easily deliver your message to both clients and new prospects.

Getting Started

If you have a type A personality, like most entrepreneurial folks I know, you'll want to jump in and do everything first. Don't do that! Skim through the book first; I made this easy to read in a few hours for that reason.

Read the material all the way through and follow the instructions as carefully as possible. You'll get a lot more from this book if you approach it with an open mind. Running a successful business takes, above all, clear and consistent vision. This is a marathon, not a sprint. You may feel that you have to get to the finish line YESTERDAY, but that's not how you run 26.2 miles - non-stop.

You first prepare and develop your plan. Read through the material first; it's not very long. You'll come back a few times to reference the various sections. Overall, you need to connect the material with your personal vision for your business.

I recommend the book for all busy entrepreneurs who want to manage their time and reach their business and personal goals.

We'll be your training partners for the length of time it takes to get you to your goal. The book will give you a foundation from which to work your plan. It will help you to keep a consistent vision of where you want to go.

Double My Revenues In 12 Months Or Less

What a Consistent Vision Can Do For You

About 15 years ago, a young man fresh out of the corporate world wanted to carve out a piece of the directory advertising business. He planned on eventually taking the venture public, but focused on starting, growing and then selling a multi-million dollar business.

After a lot of false starts, he got private equity financing and in 1980 formed the company along with his partners. The young man was singular in his vision for the company. He was criticized for not following the standard methods of operating a directory business. It wasn't easy, but TransWestern Publishing, became a leading independent publisher of yellow pages in the United States, publishing 332 directories in 25 states. In 2005, Yellow Book USA bought the company for $1.575 billion. Rick Puente walked away with roughly half a billion dollars for his vision.

Your Business as it stands now

Accounting is never usually the most exciting part of running a business (unless you're an accountant) but we're going to start there. Get your accountant or bookkeeper to work on this for you if it's too much for you to handle. Create a balance sheet to take a look at your assets and liabilities and make a profit and loss statement to see the overall picture of the health of the business. If you're just getting started in business, refer to your pro forma.

Your Business Plan.

Let's take out the business plan and review it. If you feel the need to revise it or actually make a new one, go ahead. This is the time to get it done. We need a road map if we intend to get where we're going. The plan is our road map. We intend to double whatever you've done before, but it's important to know what was done before. You'll also need to update your income/expense forecast because you'll need to see how much you can do without while you pump up your strategies for maximum effect.

The Single Page Plan

If you've been too busy to write a business plan, I've got news for you. It doesn't have to be hard and long. You can get by on a single page business plan. That's right. If you read Robert Hartung's book "Beating the Time Bandits" you will have developed your vision and that's the first step to your plan. This section explains what you do and who you'll choose to do it to or with. The foundation of your goals is laid out here.

The mission is critical.

The next step is to go back to Robert's idea of developing your mission. See how it's coming together? Your mission is the WHY of your business in the first place.

Your goals and how they relate to each other.

The goals you've laid out must now be entered to briefly explore your direction and the milestones you'll accomplish along the way. You'll want to stay away from the minute details here and go for the major accomplishments.

This is a single page plan. This part is important because you'll be tracking your progress later.

Double My Revenues In 12 Months Or Less

Which strategies will you implement and when?

Now we settle in to determine which systems and policies will be implemented to get the optimum results for reaching our goal. The standardized procedures we are developing now will allow for better tracking, easier workflow and smoother expansion of the business in the future. This part will be the basis for our turn-key system. Once you have a turn-key system, you can duplicate the business model as often as is financially feasible.

Now; the action plan,

Lay out a step by step program for the achievement of your strategies. If you find yourself adding extra pages to the plan at this point, it's fine. You've done the job you've set out to do. Congratulations!

Don't forget to review the plan on a regular basis to make improvements and track your progress.

Visit the website that details the process of creating a one page plan. http://www.onepagebusinessplan.com/

For a low cost detailed business plan template, go to these websites:

http://www.business-plan-success.com/-

A low cost business plan template website for newbies.

http://www.planware.org/index.html-

A business planning website with free and low cost software.

Your business will need additional forms for managing operational procedures; here are some links to free and low cost online forms.

Here are 12 websites that have free trial and freeware business forms for managing and keeping your business organized. I hope these websites help you to plan effectively for the upcoming chapters.

1. FreeBusinessForms.com

This is a pretty comprehensive site offering forms for almost any small business transaction. Also available on its pages is a wide-ranging list of how-to articles that offer a lot of information and insight directed at operating a successful small business.

The forms on this site can help any small business owner when they initially begin their operation. The forms designed in "Word" format require manual calculations. Those available in "Excel" format lend themselves to ready calculations and can offer a quick and easy way to crunch numbers. As time-saving tools, the downloadable forms on this site can be customized to suit your business needs.

2. Legal-Forms-Kit.com

Offers a diverse selection of forms such as an Agreement to Retain Services of an Accountant, Articles of Incorporations for a Business, Employment Agreement, and more. Also contains a comprehensive library of free information and resources for small business. An excellent resource site.

3. Smartbiz.com

The comprehensive information base, which addresses many small business owner concerns. Easy to navigate and download forms in both Excel and Word. A must-see for any small business owner or for those considering starting a small business.

4. Toolkit.cch.com

Contains lots of information for small business, including templates for model business documents. Sample letters, contracts, forms, and policies ready to be customized.

Financial spreadsheet templates. Help for managing your business finances - from balancing your checkbook to creating your own financial statements. All you need to do is plug in the numbers.

Checklists and other information at a glance - from whether you qualify for the home office write-off to the right things to do and say during an employee termination interview.

Official Government Forms. A selection of the forms and publications most commonly used by small business owners when filing taxes with the IRS or contracting with the federal government.

5. TrueHelpFinancial.com

Pretty good site, but does require that you sign up for a free membership and complete a small survey before you can download any files. However, this site contains a comprehensive information library for any small business.

6. BusinessNation.com

Variety of free forms – others for small fee. Lots of links to other business services. Pretty good resource library broken down by states.

7. HooverWebDesign.com

Good information source for anyone wanting to set up a small business web page. Good articles and some free templates. Worth checking out. Requires that you provide a link back to their page if you use any of their documentation.

8. Small Business Administration (US)

A good place to start when looking for government forms, also for connecting with some free and low-cost business consulting services.

9. CreativeBusiness.com

Some free forms, but most require payment of a small fee.

10. CreateForms.com

This website has a comprehensive list of free forms. The website does require registration.

11. www.formspring.com

This web-based form builder, website allows you to create your forms online and share them across multiple platforms. You can create forms for internal use, or place them on your website. There are options for free forms as well as a variety of monthly subscription fees.

12. www.Openoffice.org

This is the best office suite I've found anywhere. It eats up far less resources on your computer and has everything you need, except an email function to do the job. You get word processor, spreadsheet, presentation, graphics and more in a tight database driven application.

For additional email, I recommend www.yahoo.com or www.gmail.com.

Please don't think you can get by on good looks and charm. We've tried that and when those eventually failed, we had to put on the green eye-shade, roll up our sleeves and crunched the numbers. It's not how much you make; it's how much you get to keep that makes you wealthy.

The wrap-up:

Organization is paramount to the success of this program. You've got to be clear about what you want and be totally focused on your goals each day. The book "Beating the Time Bandits" is a must read before getting started. One major reason why the membership format works well for so many is the mutual support and feedback that goes with working as a group.

Your Business Model

Your competition is not the business across the street or on the other side of the world. Your competition is the 'business model' that your competition uses.

It is the way that he or she conducts business, the style, the standards, and the methods used to acquire and keep customers that makes them or you, more competitive.

The right business model holds the potential to totally innovate, renovate, and shake up your business - even an entire industry. Business models require a business plan.

The term business model describes a broad range of informal and formal models that are used by companies to represent various aspects of business, such as operational processes, organizational structures, and financial forecasts. Although the term can be traced to the 1950s, it achieved mainstream usage only in the 1990s.

A business model is the way a company plans to generate revenue and make a profit from operations. A business model includes the components and functions of the business, as well as the revenues it generates and the expenses it incurs.

For example:

A restaurant's business model is to make money by cooking and serving food to hungry customers. MacDonald's cooks and serves food to hungry people, so does Wendy's and so does the local Steak House - what they serve and how they serve, it is very different - it is their 'business model' that differentiates them and makes them competitive and appealing to a certain market segment.

A web site's business model might not be quite so clear, as there are many ways in which they can generate revenue. For example, some make money (or try to) by providing free information or service and then selling advertising to other companies who want to reach the people using the free service or information.

Then there are those who choose to sell a product or service directly to their customers when they go on-line.

Six current popular examples of current small business models are:

1. Brick and mortar
2. Franchising
3. Auctions
4. Affiliate marketing
5. Internet retail sales
6. Network marketing

Why is choosing a business model important?

Your business model defines the style, the way you plan to deliver your goods and services, and sets a standard. It becomes a touchstone, a benchmark, a way to differentiate your business from others serving the same market.

A business model defines how you plan to compete; it communicates how you create additional 'value', and becomes the magnet that draws customers whose needs are in alignment with your business model.

The process of building your business model will help you identify new opportunities, learn more about your business, and become the competition - the guy to beat.

In the process I am creating, you will likely discover something that you can use to completely transform your business. You will figure out how to break through major obstacles, discover a unique way of delivering value to the market - all which will lead you to increased sales and profits.

Business Design & Transformation

Whether you are looking to totally renovate and revolutionize your existing business or start a new business and need a blueprint for delivering a compelling customer experience - designing your business model will set you up to succeed and dominate your niche.

Then your business model becomes the tool to break through and uncover new products and services, market leadership opportunities, and the focus of your marketing and sales strategy. Here are a few examples of business models that have succeeded over the years.

- The open business model

- The subscription business model

- The razor & blades business model (bait and hook)

- The pyramid scheme business model

- The multi-level marketing business model

- The network effects business model

- The monopolistic business model

- The cutting out the middleman model

- The auction business model

- The online auction business model

- The bricks and clicks business model

- The loyalty business models

- The Collective business models

- The industrialization of services business model

- The servitization of product business model

- The low-cost carrier business model

- The online content business model

- The freemium business model

- The premium business model

- The direct sales model

- The professional open-source model

- Various distribution business models

The wrap up:

The main goal of this chapter is to get you to identify your business goals and ensure that you're using the right business model for your company. Your business model will dictate your marketing strategy. It makes little sense to pour your time, energy and money into an incompatible strategy.

Protecting Your Business

If you had a great treasure, would you leave it out in the cold and let anyone get to it without your consent? Would you leave it unprotected and vulnerable to strangers? I don't think so. We, as small business owners, already have enough challenges to face in our day to day operation.

The primary strategy for building wealth and creating the lifestyle you desire is to build an asset and create sufficient cash flow so that you can purchase other assets. That strategy is usually the creation of a business. Whether it's real estate, stock, or any product or service, you need to create a shield for assets. That shield will offer a measure of protection against civil litigation. It protects your personal assets from the risks of your business environment.

Your objective is to create a business entity that accomplishes these goals:

1. Create liability protection

2. Ensure proper asset protection

3. Maximize tax strategies

4. Optimize opportunities

5. Organize your businesses for multiple income streams

Protect Your Business Assets

Every year, millions of people overpay to the tune of billions of dollars to the IRS. The reason for this is the fact that there are over 60,000 pages in the tax code. Can your CPA keep up? Do you have a financial planner who knows your strategy and can help you to achieve it through accurate knowledge of the current tax laws?

Keep in mind that eliminating debt, cutting waste from your budget and streamlining your systems to help in doubling your revenues by increasing your cash flow for optimizing your marketing and operations. Part of that strategy must be proper and thorough tax accounting for your business.

Financial, tax, and legal protection of your business and its assets is accomplished through entity structuring. The goal of proper asset protection is to minimize your risk and to grow and sustain your asset base. The main types of entities your business can have include:

• C-Corporation: a legal entity entirely separate from the people who own the corporation. It offers over 300 deductible expenses and options for the fiscal year end date. This is a standard business corporation for-profit entity that pays taxes on the income it generates. The fiscal year is a flexible calendar system that can end at any time. Usually this ends at the regular calendar year (December 31) or after any quarter. These entities are taxed on their operating income; dividends are taxable.

Remember that the corporation is a separate entity. It is taxed and you are taxed separately on the dividends you receive. Some people call this a double tax, but remember that you are not the corporation. The corporate shield separated you and other shareholders from the business entity.

The government gives corporations a lower tax rate on the first $50,000 the company earns. (There are other tax advantages, but tax laws change annually, so you should check with your accountant for details).

A corporation acts on its own authority and files its own taxes, and it can have unlimited numbers of shareholders.

• S-Corporation: income is passed through to the shareholders of the corporation. It allows approximately 75 deductible expenses. The typical S Corp is a small business with less than 75 owners. The entity is taxed under Subchapter S of the IRS Code. The corporation pays no income tax. The IRS currently allows for about 150 allowable expense deductions and losses to flow through to the individuals.

This is a relatively new status for businesses and is still a gray area for some accountants. Find a favorable accountant who is well versed in this new business. If you are a start-up and making less than $150,000 a year or you have three or more employees, this may be the right business structure for you.

• Limited Partnership: Have one or more General Partners and one or more Limited Partners. Limited Partners share in profits, but are shielded from liabilities. General Partners have unlimited financial and legal responsibilities. Ideally, the General Partner is a C or S Corporation.

A limited partnership is to be distinguished from a general partnership, which is not a separate entity, but a pass-through to the partners, who then report their share for the profits or losses on their individual returns. The general partners are the active investors who work directly with the business. They're liable for all the financial debts and legal obligations.

There is also a limited partnership entity for family businesses called an FLP. Family Limited Partnerships (FLPs) are limited partnerships where the majority of the partners are family members.

• Limited Liability Company (LLC): a separate entity for asset protection purposes. If sued, only the assets of the LLC (not the people) are at risk. It is a type of organization called a hybrid entity. LLCs combine the best of both partnerships and corporations. You get the corporate shield of a limited form of liability protection and pass-through taxation to the business owners.

The members of the LLC also receive the partnership-like advantage of pass-through taxation or elect to be taxed a C corporation.

• Trusts: removes property from the reach of creditors and unwelcome beneficiaries.

The wrap up:

Your goal should be to work with a tax strategist or CPA to maximize your tax deductions while limiting your personal liability.

It's very important to have your team in place for all your business needs. You will need to have legal, accounting, operational, marketing and logistics support.

The Message Clutter

April 2004: A Yankelovich Partners poll for the American Association of Advertising concluded that consumers believed they are constantly bombarded with advertising.

61% said that advertising was out of control.

60% said that they had a negative opinion of advertising.

54% said that they avoided buying products that overwhelm them with ads.

How do you overcome the Message Clutter?

Carefully select your buyers.

Educate your prospective clients.

Entertain them.

Focus on referrals

Make them an offer they can't refuse.

If you could build the ideal profile of your best client, what would they be like? Can you clearly envision the result of a transaction with your ideal client?

List 10 traits of your ideal client then determine how many of them you can realistically service each month.

Do the math to calculate your conversion rate. If you actively presented your business to 100 prospective clients, how many could you convert to paying clients for your product or service in a month? Is there an opportunity to generate repeat business from these clients? What is the buying cycle for your average client?

Let's take your answers to the next step.

For example:

Our Dentist has an average per patient rate of $3200. 00 a year. He wants to double his patient roster and introduce several new products this year.

He currently sees 100 patients a month. The number of patients that currently fit his ideal profile is about 40 a month. He determines that an additional 20 ideal patients a month would make his goal a reality. Now he must find them.

Educate your clients.

Now that we have an idea of who we need to reach, let's get to reaching them.

Let's be clear about this fact. People might hate being sold to, but they all want more information on what to buy. They want to be educated.

People are interested in knowing more about the things that interest them. If they can get the right information at the right time, they will be in a great position to take action in their interest.

Entertain them.

When you want to stand out, you can make an impression with your audience by inserting humor into your presentations. Humor leaves a lasting impression.

Focus on Referrals

Another way to circumvent the message clutter is to petition your current clients for referrals. There are ways to do this without begging. One way is to combine education and referral strategies – Invite your clients to a seminar and offer an incentive to bring a few friends.

Make them an offer they can't refuse.

This is not just a tactic of gangster movies. If you search thoroughly through the feature, advantages and benefits of your offer, you can find one unique area that will undeniably appeal to your market. If you show them how they cannot lose by using you or your product then they will move to act in their own self-interest.

Create offers that not only give top notch value, but also appropriate information. Give them an iron clad guarantee. There must be something in your offer that shows how confident you are in what you have or do.

The wrap up:

Get your message to the right target audience.

The most important practice in marketing is getting the message to the people who welcome it as an opportunity, not an interruption. We found that education elevates your message to another level.

The Magnificent 7

Essential tools for your marketing and sales

1. Advertising

2. Public Relations

3. Direct Mail

4. Personal Sales

5. Internet

6. Print Promotions

7. Education

The way to use these powerful tools is through a synergistic strategy. I've found that the most successful businesses have at least five of the seven tools working for their business daily. Now, depending on your type of business, some tools will be more effective than others; use the tools with the end goal in mind. By carefully matching the tools to your goals, you'll find the right marketing mix for your business.

1. Advertising

Advertising is the practice of using the paid media to build a brand or create awareness.

This vast practice is often misunderstood my small business owners who use the "let's throw it against the wall and see what sticks strategy" for advertising success.

Advertising in itself does not make a sale. It can create demand or awareness for a product or service. If money were no object, advertising would be a lot easier. You could try one medium at a time or all media at once, then track them for results. The fact is that you don't have unlimited resources. You need to have an advertising campaign that clearly outlines the objectives of the program and the tracking mechanisms for evaluating the program.

If you are a service company, your needs will be different from a manufacturing or retail company. If your model is business to business, your strategies will be different from a business to consumer model. Let's look at a few standard media selections:

Direct mail

If you are a small business, direct mail is the best bet for ramping up quality leads in a short time. You can create a direct response program for targeting a small test market and expand from there as your results come in.

Radio

The reasonable alternative for broadcast advertising

Double My Revenues In 12 Months Or Less

You can get a branding boost – this tactic is more suited for the broad range lead generation. Radio in conjunction with website and targeted direct mail promotions are a classic mix for both Business to Business and Business to Consumers companies.

Television

This is the medium for building your image. You can create a lot of buzz with television advertising. Like radio, you can build a strategy that uses the power of Television to draw the public into your direct response medium. This is a very expensive medium.

Magazines

This form of print advertising is not as great a medium for image advertising as the more expensive Television model. The ability to reach a niche market through specialized magazine publications is the primary advantage of magazines when compared to radio and newspapers. This medium works with both B to B and B to C models.

Newspapers

This medium offers an effective local presence for promotions. People who use the newspapers and circulars as a means of local advertising will find that circulation in most areas have been drastically reduced. People are reading less in print and reading more on the Internet. Newspapers are gaining more ad revenue online each year and steadily moving their content to the Internet. For a quick, direct response advertising program, newspapers offer an efficient way of testing and lead generation.

Print Promotion

From business cards to door knockers, flyers , postcards, print promotions are a staple for small business startups. Many use these quick and dirty promotional tools to market their products and services in conjunction with newspaper advertising. The tactic works for B to B as well as B to C companies.

Yellow Pages

This tactic is technically not advertising, but direct response marketing. People tend to go to the directories; the directories do not go to them. The covers act as advertising, but the information sought by the consumer is what builds the value of the directory. When we use the directories, we choose the advertiser that most closely fits the solution to our problem. Use the yellow pages in conjunction with the Internet to solidify your message.

Signage

A local tool for branding, signage directs local business prospects to your business like nothing else can. Signage gives your company a strong emotional contact with your prospects. There is a sense of integrity that comes with a well-designed sign program.

2. Public Relations

PR professionals are always coming up with clever ideas for getting their clients noticed, especially in the form of free and powerful publicity. Public relations include networking, speeches and personal appearances. These activities are not sales tactics, they lay the groundwork.

Keep in mind that your goal is still to attract the public's attention in a way that will draw the ones who need your help to seek you out.

3. Direct mail

Use this strategy to reach highly targeted prospects on a consistent basis. The power of direct mail is in the list you use. You must be absolutely certain that the prospects on your list have a keen interest in your offer.

4. Personal Sales

Did you know that it costs more than seven times as much to get a new customer as it does to keep an existing one? That fact in itself should help you to understand the value of building a relationship with your existing customers and turning into both repeat buyers and spokespeople for your company.

5. Internet

The fastest growing medium for effective and efficient marketing is the World Wide Web. A website and online marketing program are indispensable tools for generating new business and managing existing clients.

6. Print Promotions

Whether you are designing an ad or creating sales collateral, print promotions are at the heart of much of your marketing strategy. The goal of your print promotions must be clearly defined before initiating a program.

7. Education

The most successful companies offer their clients useful information that empowers them to change their lives for the better. The value of a satisfied and loyal customer is priceless. Offering free information that is of benefit to prospects and clients creates greater Top of Mind Awareness and enhances the loyalty of the people you reach.

The wrap up:

Use the above list to choose your most appropriate combination of marketing tools. Decide how much time, energy and money you can afford to invest in your marketing strategy.

The Five Fingers of Marketing Success

How do you use these tools for maximum effectiveness? Look at your hand. If you have five fingers on your hand, (most of us do) you now have the best strategic resource reminder possible.

Choose five of the seven marketing tools that fit your business model. Set up a rotation strategy for your marketing. Here are the steps for making a determination.

First, are you basically a service company or a product based company?

Are you a business to business company, or basically a business to consumer based company? The most powerful tactic in your group is represented by the thumb. It does a lot of work and complements the power of the four fingers. Your little pinky finger represents the least powerful but very useful weapon in your arsenal. Use this analogy to visualize the combined power of your marketing tactic as a fist knocking out the competition.

Here are the basic marketing techniques that have the highest probability of success for each business model.

Service To Consumers

Mentors / Gatekeepers-

Business Branding-

Radio and TV-

Magazine, Newspaper Publicity-

Incentives Discount Pricing-

Circulars and Fliers-

Yellow Page Ads-

Bulletin Boards-

Tear Sheets-

Radio Show-

Podcast-

Web site-

Membership Site-

Blog-

Books-

Webinars-

Service For Business

Personal Contact-

Networking-

Double My Revenues In 12 Months Or Less

Mentors-

Volunteering-

Charity-

Referrals-

Business Cards-

Articles-

Newsletters-

Trade Publications-

Publicity-

Seminars-

Sampling-

Web site-

Webinars-

Books-

Online Training-

Podcasts-

Service / Product

Sales To Consumers-

Mentors / Gatekeepers-

Consumer Branding-

Radio and TV-

Magazine-

Newspaper-

Publicity-

Incentives-

Discount Pricing-

Circulars and Fliers-

Direct Mail-

Yellow Page Ads-

Bulletin Boards-

Tear Sheets-

Radio Show-

Television Show-

Podcast-

Web site-

Membership Site-

Blogs-

Books-

Webinars-

Double My Revenues In 12 Months Or Less

Service / Product Sales To Business

Personal Contact – Mentors / Gatekeepers

Volunteering – Charity

Referrals Business Cards – Articles

Publicity - Business Publications

Sampling - Demonstrations

Business Directories – Website

Webinar – E-Book

Online Training

Podcast

Products To Consumers

Mentors / Gatekeepers

Product Packaging

Point Of Sale Display – Sampling

Incentives - Discount Pricing

Giveaways – Direct Mail

Classified Ads – Own TV Show – Direct

Response Ads Podcast – Website

Membership Site – Blog – E-Book

Webinars

Products To Businesses

Personal Contact – Networking - Mentors

Volunteering – Charity – Referrals

Business Cards – News Releases

Business Trade Publications

Sampling – Webinars

Demonstrations

Business Directories

Membership Site

Blog – Books

The wrap up:

If you need to remember anything about the strategies of marketing it's this; never rely on one or two tactical tools to do the job of increasing your revenues.

Think of it as the 5 Fingers of Marketing Success.

Getting Your Site on Page One

Marketing your services or products on the Internet is no longer a luxury even for local businesses. If you are not on page ONE for your significant buying keywords you are leaving money on the table and giving it all to your competition. There was a time when a small business owner could get by on placing ads in the Yellow Pages or investing in local newspaper advertising; those days are gone.

The Power Of The Web

Like electricity, telephones and talk radio; the Internet has become ubiquitous. The vast majority of Americans make use of the Internet at least once a week. The World Wide Web is no longer just a refuge for nerds and geeks. The information superhighway is now a utility used by almost everyone, even my mother.

Small business owners must learn how to utilize the web for lead generation and sales conversion. This knowledge is important for long-term growth. It's not necessary to be an expert in search engine optimization or search marketing; a business owner just needs to know what it will take to stay competitive online. Let me show you 6 easy steps to getting online leads on autopilot.

You don't need to learn how search engines work to make a profit from them. You will need to know what it will take to put you in the front of the line in as many search terms as you will need to drive targeted traffic to your offer. Before I get into that, however, let me stress to you the importance of search engines in terms of today's marketplace.

Search engines are now the primary local information source for US consumers. For the first time, search engines have trumped printed yellow pages for local information. More customers than ever are using the web to find businesses; and, online searchers are more likely to convert to buyers even offline.

Okay, you understand the need for being on the Internet because you're reading this short report. Let's take a look at why you need to be on the first page for a search term or keyword relating to your offer. Many small business owners set up a website and move on with their daily activities. For some, the website is just like a business card or sign.

I think you understand by now the importance of having a web presence, but is your site or blog set up properly to accommodate both the search engines and your visitors? We're going to cover the first steps to page One; keyword research.

Why Keyword Research Is Important - The Short Version

When using the Internet to generate leads, you are looking at a specific market. Your market is a community of people who share a common interest in a particular subject or activity. Your market will use specific keywords and phrases to look for what they want in relation to your service or product.

When you market on the web, you are trying to attract a community based on their search habits. In order to do that effectively, you need to understand the language that they use. People who play golf use far different terms for their interests than those who play Dungeons & Dragons.

Many of the languages that are specific to each market will appear in search terms as keywords or phrases. Within the market, you will find multiple niches that relate to the overall market and its community. A niche is a subset of a market relating to a specific topic. Think of the market as a book and the niches as chapters within the book.

For example, members of the martial arts market will be interested in a wide range of topics relating to martial arts. These might include:

- Tae Kwon Do

- Praying Mantis Kung Fu

- Martial Arts Weapons Training

- Karate Uniforms

- Wing Chun Kung Fu

- Judo Clubs

- Martial Arts Films

- Ninja Throwing Stars

Each of the above topics can be considered a niche within the overall market. Each niche may have specific keywords and phrases unique to its subject. Let's take a quick look at how people choose keywords when conducting searches. No two people will conduct a search exactly the same way. Two martial artists looking for tae kwon do uniforms, may do so in a completely different manner.

One person may be looking for "tae kwon do uniform styles and designs". Another person may prefer to look for "cool martial arts uniforms for tae kwon do". Go to Google and enter those two keyword phrases and you'll notice very different results. You'll also notice the difference in the number of searches for each inquiry.

One keyword phrase may generate a lot more traffic to a website than another. This tends to place a different value on each keyword search term. This means that the biggest factors in your success in marketing online will be based on the market you choose and the keywords you target. Getting these two factors right will significantly influence your income.

Most people don't spend the time to do the research necessary to find the right keywords to unlock their profits. They don't target keywords at all on their website or in their marketing efforts. Those who succeed online will conduct careful research into the overall market, various profitable niches within the market and target specific keyword phrases.

The wrap up:

Online markets are communities of people who share an interest in a particular subject and often have their own way of describing their experiences, wants and needs.

There can be many niches within a market. Each niche represents specific topics of interest to members within that market.

Keywords and phrases are vital to unlocking the profits within a niche. Different keywords have different levels of importance depending on the amount of traffic they generate.

Choosing the right market and picking the right keywords and phrases within a niche are probably the two most important aspects of successful online marketing.

Keyword Research Tools - Winning The Battle For Page One

Keyword research helps you to gain insight into what your prospects want, what they're concerned about and what they need. Google's awesome keyword research tool no longer exists, however. In its place is the Google AdWords Planner, which is not as good or as flexible as its previous incarnation. You will need to have a Google AdWords account in order to use it. You can try these free online options.

Free Keyword Research Tools:

WordStream Keyword Tool

Wordtracker

SEO Book Keyword Tool

Double My Revenues In 12 Months Or Less

Ubersuggest

Keyword Eye

Soovle

YouTube Keyword Tool

Market Samurai (free version)

For the sake of simplicity and brevity, I'm not going to go into an in-depth explanation of each free keyword tool. Take some time to click on the links and explore each one to see how they can help you. Each tool is different in their approach to keyword research, but they are an excellent way to get started.

There are paid tools as well free tools available. Once you have a working understanding of keyword research you'll know how to find relevant keywords, and find high-traffic keywords as well as low and medium competition keywords.

Here Are The Six Simple Steps To Page One Ranking

1.   Thoroughly research your market to ensure that you are pointed in the right direction.

2.   Research the appropriate (relevant) keywords relating to your specific niche within the chosen market.

3.   Establish high-traffic keywords versus low traffic keywords - find out the cost involved in competing. Choose a combination of low competition and medium competition keywords (about 10 should work).

4.   Assess the market competition and commercial intent for your chosen keywords to see what it's going to take to achieve page one for each keyword phrase.

5.   Optimize your website and content strategically for your keyword phrases.

6.   Determine your traffic strategy for driving visitors using your keyword phrases. Link building, Advertising, Social Networking; do it.

That's it. Successful Internet marketing is as simple as that. Of course, simple, doesn't always mean easy. Time, patience and practice is usually needed to get things to work properly, consistently and efficiently.

Double My Revenues In 12 Months Or Less

Each phase of the operation requires multiple steps. Take the time to learn and get good at one of the various phases and outsource the rest. My recommendation is to get really good at keyword research.

It is important to find keywords that have enough traffic to be worth targeting. A really easy keyword to rank on page one may bring one visitor a year! You may spend a lot of money on a high-traffic keyword phrase, gain a lot of traffic but no conversions. The commercial potential for a keyword phrase is also important to your overall goal.

Now that you have an idea of what it takes to rank on the first page of Google, Bing and Yahoo; as well as any other search engine let's get back to keywords. I know, you're probably wondering why you have to read more about keywords. The answer is, because it's important to your income. You are about to learn the secret to making those previous six simple steps work for you consistently.

Keyword Research Best Practices Revealed

When doing your research, look for these four essential elements:

- Niche Relevance

- Traffic Potential

- Online Competition

- Commercial Potential

The first step is to generate a large (make that humongous) list of keywords relating to your niche. The next step is to filter the good keywords from the list. What you're looking for are keywords that:

- Have relevance

- Offer good traffic potential

- Present manageable competition

- Show commercial value

What; did you hear about that list before? That's right, it is so important that I repeated myself. The reason for this is because you need to understand and identify the profitable and accessible keywords to target for your business. Your chosen keywords must fit the four criteria posted above (twice for emphasis).

Niche Relevance

This refers to finding keywords that reaches the right target audience who are willing to make a commitment to your offer. Find the keywords that are most relevant to the subject matter of your website. Many people who get into in-depth keyword research are amazed at some of the hidden results. They often come across words and phrases that are overlooked; buried gold nuggets.

Traffic Potential

Double My Revenues In 12 Months Or Less

One of the great dilemmas of keyword research and search marketing in general relates to choosing the appropriate keywords for marketing goals. Over 90% of all keywords within a given niche have insignificant levels of traffic. Most of these are not worth spending a lot of time and money to rank.

Although everyone seems to have their own ideas regarding an ideal traffic generating keyword, let's set a parameter of 30 visitors a day for the number one spot on the first page. We're going to use this benchmark for traffic potential while keeping one important fact in mind; it's usually not easy to get to the number one slot. Take a look at the stats shown above regarding first page search engine traffic.

Remember that the vast majority of searches is completed on page One! If no one searches page 20, there is no value in being there. This is why it is so important to do the research necessary to ensure that you can compete with others to get to the first page of the search engines.

There is usually a list of relevant keywords that are worth investigating because they offer fairly significant levels of targeted traffic yet are relatively cheap to rank on page one. For the sake of simplicity, let's choose the 10 best phrases that fit all four parameters. Your goal is to be able to rank far enough on page one for each phrase to generate enough Web traffic to gain profitable conversions… consistently.

Online Competition

Let's face it, some words and phrases are going to be too expensive to be worth the effort of competing for the first page. In order to find out which ones are suitable, you'll need to determine the strengths of the competition for each keyword. Take your top 10 chosen keyword phrases and begin a search in Google for each one. Take note of the website links from the first page. Disregard the advertising on the page for now. Collect the URLs of each site on the second page as well. Your goal is to find out how powerful these pages are and whether you can beat them.

Many keyword research tools (Market Samurai, Longtail Keyword Pro, etc.) offer assistance in competitive analysis. It is important to know before you commit whether or not you can afford to take on your competition for a specific keyword phrase. Consider the two most important aspects of keyword competition when conducting your evaluation.

Strength Of Competition And Amount Of Competition

The relative strength of your competitors refers to their ability to impress the heck out of Google and retain their elite position on page one. In a highly competitive arena this can be difficult and costly but also rewarding. Strive to build your website's authority with content and relevant backlinks.

Amount of competition refers to the number of websites clamoring to get on page one. Don't be afraid to go after keywords with a high amount of competition if the strength of the competition is weaker than your optimized page.

If the top 10 spots on a given page, are dominated by corporate owned websites with a national presence and lots of relevant content, this might not be the right keyword for you. For example, a realtor in a local market might be up against all the national companies such as Zillow, Century 21, Realtor.com and others.

If, however, the bottom half of that page displays a local website for a realtor who, upon closer inspection can be knocked off with a few advanced SEO techniques, then there is a possibility of getting to page one. Maintaining your position may not be that easy however.

Knowing the strength of competition for a given keyword phrase and determining whether you can afford to get to page one with it is an important step in keyword research. Let's face it, some battles just aren't meant to be fought. The good news is that there are plenty of low competition or medium competition keywords within a given niche that have enough traffic potential to be profitable.

When you're assessing the competition on the first page for a given keyword in Google, start with a top ranking site. Look to see if the title of the page closely corresponds to the keyword you're shooting for.

Look at the short description that Google previews under the title. You're looking to see if your keyword phrase shows up in these two areas.

If your competition for all 10 spots have both titles and description displaying your keywords in the proper order, you know that they are applying search engine optimization principles. You can continue on to page 2 in order to see how many additional competitors are trying to actively go after this keyword.

If you find that you are moving on to page 3 because page 2 is filled with optimized pages then you may want to take a look at another keyword. But we're not done yet! We have looked at the number of competitors, but we haven't evaluated their strength.

One of the quickest ways to determine the strength of your competition is to take a look at their page rank and the number of backlinks they've accumulated as well as their Alexa ranking. There are other factors such as domain authority and trust authority, but for now let's keep it simple.

If you use Firefox as your browser you can go to the add-on section in your setup tab and choose SEOquake. This handy little add-on will allow you to gain a lot of insight into your competitors' pages. I won't go into the full instructions on how to utilize it here because SEOquake offers very good instructions on how to use their plug-in.

Once the plug-in is installed, you can go through each of the ranking pages to see if they have a lot of strength. You can even take a look at the page info provided by the plug-in to get detailed information on page ranking, age of the domain, keyword density, internal and external linking structure and many other pieces of information.

This is a handy free tool for spying on the competition and even learning how to alter the content of your own page to be more successful. Try it on your own site to see how you stack up against the competition. You'll want to ensure that your webpage is properly optimized before your link building campaign begins.

If you learn to assess the relative strength of the competition properly, you will be able to know what it will take to get to page one and beat out many seemingly tough competitors such as online directories, Yelp and even some national chains. It will still take a lot of work and diligence to stay in the top 10.

You can save yourself a lot of frustration (and money) by applying keyword research thoroughly at the start of your campaign. Ideally, this should be done before you even design a website or blog. Once you make it a habit to look at the page info of your competitors you'll begin to see a pattern.

Commercial Intent of Keywords

What if you got the keywords you want to rankono page one and got a lot of traffic, but no one bought from you? You might blame your website offer or the power of your sales letter but there might be one simple reason; the commercial potential of the keyword is very low. What you need to consider is whether other people are getting leads from this keyword phrase.

One way to determine the commercial value of your keyword is to look at the search engines again. Are there ads running on the page? Go to Google AdWords or Bing and Yahoo and check if similar ads are being run there as well. Find out how much the ads are going for and how competitive the space is for that keyword in Pay Per Click.

Getting all the other factors right and neglecting commercial intent leads to frustration and low profits. Take the extra step to find out if your keyword phrases are going to make you money.

Laying Out The Perfect Scenario

Let's take a look at the ideal scenario for keyword research and its application in search engine marketing. Let's say you're selling a health product online; you're about to create the website and you decide to do a little research to find the perfect set of keywords to generate 5,000 visitors a month.

Many experienced online marketers have used the rule of thumb they call the 1%. They've estimated that one out of 100 visitors to a decent website will take action on offer. Your goal of 5,000 visitors a month would give you roughly 166 visitors a day.

You find 10 keywords from a long list that are relevant to your market niche, roughly calculates to 30,000 visitors a month combined and is a mixture of low competition and medium competition. One final check reveals that the chosen 10 also have a medium to high commercial intent. Now at last you're ready to use these 10 keywords on your website.

Since you're using WordPress for your web platform, you make sure that the title tags on all your pages match your main keywords. You fill in the meta-descriptions with associated keyword phrases. Your meta-descriptions include your main keyword in different variations so as not to over optimize your page.

Each of your pages should have an image with an associated keyword close to your main keyword phrase in the image tag and you sprinkle various other keywords from your search (high, low, and medium competitive) in the article as well. I like to add a video as well that relates to the topic.

Once you feel that you have your main pages properly optimized, it's time to create internal links between your pages. These internal links will help to spread the link potential throughout your website. Look for keywords and phrases through each page that can be associated with another page on your site and link to them. Each page should also have a link to your main page as well from an anchor text.

To give your pages some authority, be sure to add an external link to an authority site, such as Wikipedia or an authority in the niche you are promoting. This external link should be no follow. Search engines like authority and will see your page as valuable if it contains links to other authority sites.

Once you've completed all the optimization, you may find that your pages have started to climb in the rankings automatically once you index them. A properly optimized page should not need a lot of external backlinks to start ranking properly in the search engines.

The wrap up:

There are four very important factors to consider in choosing your keywords:

- Niche Relevance

- Traffic Potential

- Online Competition

- Commercial Potential

Be sure that your website is optimized for your keywords before link building and promotion begins.

Double My Revenues In 12 Months Or Less

Let's discuss the link building process in detail now that we've covered keyword research and its application. By now you should be aware that creating links to your site from other sites is called backlinking. Search engines equate the quality of the link that comes from another site to yours as an endorsement of your content.

Links with your keyword embedded in the anchor text from another site has the potential of being noticed and accounted for by search engine robots. Unfortunately, Google has become sensitive to spam links and will penalize websites using "black hat' techniques. The truth is that all SEO is "black hat". Optimization for ranking your site is "artificial" and not the natural progression of site popularity.

In the past, webmasters and search engine marketers have tried a variety of strategies to gain links from other sites. There have been a mad rush to accumulate back links in order to gain rankings. "The greater the number of back links, the greater the chances of getting to Page One!"

The Trouble With Back Links

If you do this kind of competitive analysis long enough, you'll begin to see several strange things. You might find that a prominent page has achieved a lot of power and ranking without showing a lot of backlinks leading to it. Many people are still under the impression that the more backlinks you have, the better your shot at hitting page one. This isn't necessarily true; as a matter of fact it's misleading.

71

Search engines evaluate the page according to a number of factors. Although the page rank of the site does influence the individual pages their relevance and the relevance of the backlinks to them are also important. Many of the factors that go into ranking a page are kept hidden in the search engine algorithm. What we do know is that on-page optimization and backlinking are two areas under our control.

The process of backlinking is supposed to be a measure of a website's esteem. Others come to your page, find it useful and link to it so that many others may benefit from your wisdom. This essentially is the core idea of linking one website page to another. However, having 10,000 low level backlinks won't help a web page to gain rankings against one that has 10 super powered backlinks from 10 different authority sites.

It is especially disastrous for someone to create a new website and pay someone five dollars to pound the crap out of it with thousands of spam backlinks from foreign countries in a matter of days. Since

Google loves to change the rules of the game every so often, it's probably a good idea to stay conservative and look for quality instead of quantity when it comes to backlinking and optimization.

At this point in time, an effective strategy for adding backlinks to your webpage requires a multi-tiered system. Your main website gains links from a tier 1 network of websites that include links from the following:

- Article Directories - Ezinearticles.Com

- Web 2.0 Pages – Wordpress.Com

- Wiki Sites

- Pdf Document Sites

- Video Sites – Youtube.Com

- Social Networking Sites – Facebook.Com

- Microblogs – Twitter

- Image Sites

- Profile Links

Building Your Tier 1 Network Back Link System

Your tier 1 network should have a healthy supply of backlinks from a variety of these sources. I have included a bonus file with the list of top ranking web 2.0 sites to link your webpages. You can outsource this effort if you don't want to do it yourself.

Once this is done, you can begin to send backlinks to your tier 1 level. This would become your Tier 2 level. Tier 2 will require more automated back linking because there will be more sites to get to. Programs such as SEnuke X CR and GSA Search Engine Ranker can build backlinks almost on autopilot to your tier 1 and tier 2 networks.

The next step is to bolster your top tiers with more back links; build a tier 3, tier 4 and tier 5 level to fully establish the power of your site. This will give authority to the entire structure of your back linking system. This is how you compete with the people who are spending a lot of money to get to page One.

Keeping The Competition At Bay

How long will you have to do this in order to achieve your goal? That depends on your goal, obviously. If you're looking to build a list of leads that convert to sales you'll have to determine what your leads are worth in terms of time and money. Getting the traffic is only the first step; you'll need to convert that traffic into your final objective. If you have a lot of competition than the work may be more strenuous or expensive.

Establishing quality backlinks can take a lot of work. There is one secret technique that many STO experts have kept from their customers for a long time. This strategy is just now surfacing in the mainstream. Private Blog networks (PBN) have been around for quite some time in various forms. These networks of blogs I specifically designed to generate high page rank authority back links.

Double My Revenues In 12 Months Or Less

Instead of having thousands and thousands of low quality backlinks to your site, having one or two high page rank, high authority backlinks along with your web 2.0 tier structure helps to push you ahead of the crowd. You can use these high-powered links on your main site to quickly give it authority.

Renting Authority Backlinks

You can spend the money to establish your own private blog network or you can purchase high authority backlinks without the expense and hassle of trying to set up and maintain the network yourself. Either way, you can have specific anchor texts pointing from a high authority site to your page helping it to rank in a matter of days or weeks instead of months for a given keyword.

Private Blog Networks

High authority sites are expensive. When you build them yourself, you're going to need a hosting account with separate IP addresses for each of your sites. PBNs are made up of high page rank, aged high authority domains. You can purchase these from various sources, including GoDaddy.com and other companies that sell aged domains.

When setting up a PBN, you will need to conduct a thorough check of each domain name to ensure that its ranking is authentic and its existing backlinks are clean and not filled with junk. You can go to majesticSEO.com to check the authority level of the domain name and http://checkpagerank.net/ to ensure that the page rank is genuine. Both of these sites offer free access to basic information.

If you don't want to go through the trial and error and expense of building your own private blog network, contact me about setting one up if you are interested. They do take a lot of work because they need relevant content as well as link building to maintain their authority.

The wrap up:

More backlinks is not always a good thing. Protect your main site with several tiers of backlinks to ensure that you don't get penalized by the search engines. Think quality and relevance over quantity. Private Blog networks (PBN) can help to bring quality backlinks to a page and help it rank quickly. Renting high authority backlinks can level the playing field and bring your site to page one.

Tracking Your Progress

"You won't know if you got there if you don't know where you're going and you won't know if you succeeded if you don't know where you are." This tortured saying is very true when it comes to search engine marketing. Not only do you need to start out with a plan, you need a way to track your progress. There are a number of SEO programs to help you track your stats.

If you're short on money, here are a couple of places I consider essential for keeping track of your website properties.

MajesticSEO can help you evaluate your position in terms of domain authority.

Serpfox can help you establish your tracking system for ranking.

Internetmarketingninjas has a variety of free tools that can be accessed from this link.

There are plenty of paid programs available as well to help you analyze and track your ranking statistics. I definitely recommend paying the extra fee for Serpfox when you are tracking several websites and wish to generate reports. The monthly cost is fairly inexpensive compared to other online services.

Programs like Market Samurai and online services like Moz and MajesticSEO can certainly help to track your website's progress while helping to develop its library of profitable keywords. If you're reading this and you feel that you have started off in a totally different direction (one that is not working for you) don't scratch everything. Start with keyword research to ensure that you have the right market, the right niche, good traffic potential, decent competitive opportunity and good profit potential.

Last Words On The Subject

We covered quite a lot in this chapter; from the value of thorough keyword research to the importance of understanding the competition. Evaluating a keyword's value is not a hard and fast practice; more keywords and phrases are coming on board every day as more people use the web to find what they're looking for. The popularity of some keywords rise and fall within a year.

One thing you can be sure of; if you are targeting a medium or a high competitive keyword phrase you will need to be prepared for the constant fluctuation of your position in the marketplace. There will definitely be others looking to outrank you. Your site's position will no doubt go up and down throughout the weeks therefore do not panic!

This is one reason why it is a good idea to keep an eye on your valuable keywords to see when you may need to bolster the authority of a keyword that seems to be stuck or moving backwards. As you become more experienced at picking quality keywords with traffic potential and reasonable competitiveness you can begin to rank for harder keywords as you build more niche authority and more traffic.

Making Massive Profits with E-mail Lists

In this era of spam (and I mean endless spam), many web marketers are very leery of e-mail marketing. The U.S. CAN-SPAM Act has made it very dangerous for spamming in the U.S.; most ethical marketers don't intentionally use spam anyway. So how can people use e-mail safely these days to create wealth?

The only good list is a clean list.

What is a clean list? A clean list is one with no outdated or un-formatted addresses. A clean list will have a higher rate of accurate delivery. This means more messages are delivered correctly to the target audience. The quickest way to tick off your Internet Service Provider is to have a large rate of bounce back e-mail addresses.

If you had a clean list, they are less likely to block your e-mail messages or send them to the spam folders. Your level of concern will be vastly different if you had a list of 60 versus a list of 60,000. You'll need to clean your list if you e-mail from it often.

Staying ahead of the curve

Whenever possible, use a service like Aweber, GetResponse or Icontact for your e-mail marketing. It's a lot easier to manage and though they are subscription based, they make the job of e-mail marketing a whole lot simpler.

Perhaps the biggest reason to use a service is the changing legal landscape and technology. It's hard to keep up with the various trends in technology and legal affairs, you and I have businesses to run. The other reason is the rise in e-mail monitoring systems that hunt for spammers. The more you e-promote, the greater your chance of being monitored.

These services watch e-mail deliveries and will put your e-mail address or mail server identification number on their lists if they suspect you. ISPs and other e-mail services consult these blacklists to help them decide whether to allow, block, or filter your messages.

Check your e-promotion reports after each session to find out who is blocking you. Several of my clients have had their services blocked by a large provider like Juno. Your IT/database people or your e-mail company can work with the ISPs and blacklists to resolve disputes.

You may need to change the way you send messages - and get very serious about monitoring who you send your messages to. If you currently run all your e-mails through your own computer, change to a service.

If you currently use a service and are having issues, do a little research and switch to another. Most e-mail plans start around $24.00 a month.

How much is too much?

I tend to live by the seven day rule. There is a delicate balance to e-promoting, I follow the same rule of thumb for e-mail that I do for phone marketing. If I initiate contact with a person this week, unless it's absolutely necessary, I wait until the same day next week to try again. Unless a person tries to get in touch with me, and gives me permission to re-contact that person before the seven day period is up.

This avoids e-mail burnout, irritated prospects and possible loss of future profits. The rule of seven days seems to work well because the passing of a weekend seems to mark an acceptable time period in most people's minds. In any event, carefully gauge your prospect's tolerance for communication.

This Is As Simple As It Gets

I promised to make this a very simple process for generating targeted traffic and converting an average of 60% of that traffic to paying customers.

The exact order of actions that must occur to create maximum online sales in today's market are as follows:

* Identify your niche market and collect at least 100 keyword phrases.

* Research your niche and identify at least 5 to 10 sub-niche markets.

* Get a reliable web host and a domain name that references your market.

* Get a commercial auto-responder service.

* Write at least 10 keyword rich articles for each sub niche market.

* Write 20 follow-up emails for your auto-responder for each of your sub- niches. You will be building a communication pipeline to your leads.

* Create a keyword optimized, benefits-rich squeeze page for each sub- niche. The reason you'll want to create more than one will be shown.

* Drive traffic to the squeeze pages to build targeted email lists using 5 tactics. You won't be relying on just one method, I'll tell you why.

* Develop an ongoing relationship with the subscribers on your email lists.

* Send a monthly survey to your email lists to find out what they want and need. This is the heart of great marketing – get at the truth.

* As you convert subscribers to customers, establish a separate strategy for them. You definitely must treat your customers differently.

* Create products that exactly meet the needs of your customers.

* Build more high dollar products and services into your business model.

That's it. That's all there is to it. As I said, it is very simple. The problem is that most people want to make it more complicated because they don't trust simplicity. If you are one of those people, I'll make it more complex by giving you more details. Keep reading.

If you don't have a website and are looking to get into business online, I can give you a few ideas on how to succeed without a traditional website. Of course, this depends on your market and your business model. I personally have too many websites and at some time in the future, will have to simplify my business.

If you feel that you are out of your league in any of the areas we covered above, let me know what you need. I can offer you the appropriate services to fit your needs, so that you can concentrate on the areas you are most proficient in at this time.

I also offer one-on-one and group coaching. If this is more appealing to you, just go to this link and we'll set up a time for a free phone evaluation. It's easy once you know your market and the potential of it. It gets tough when everything seems so uncertain. Having someone to get you through the briar patch of starting up really does make the process a whole lot easier and more enjoyable.

Let's face it, even Tiger Woods and other amazing people have coaches and mentors. If you are doing this to make an above average income, you'll need to invest in it properly. I coach my clients from a practical standpoint, no theory, no fluff. Go to my coaching page for more information.

Create an online marketing plan to convert 60% of your leads traffic to customers

Too many online businesses skip this step; even the established business owners who should know better. They see their website as an afterthought.

1.   The first rule of successful marketing planning – Only sell something you know has a proven track record of attracting willing buyers with the money and a strong desire for the product or service you offer.

Before you create or select your product, go to Google or Yahoo and check the popularity of your ideas. Go to several online book sources, including Amazon, Borders and eBay to research the availability of your product. Once you've decided that the product you've chosen has a market that satisfies your needs, create or purchase the rights to your first product.

2.   Think long term -- plan for a series of similar products that will service your customer base for the long haul. The product line must be useful and worthwhile for your customers and be able to translate into ongoing sales. For instance, if you're selling an herbal remedy for weight loss, have at least four associated products to up-sell and a few free giveaways.

Establish a plan for creating a monthly email newsletter for your prospects and customers. The key to long term growth is consistent communication and follow up. Now, you'll need to gather enough of your market to make the project worthwhile.

That means gathering a list. There are many ways to compile your list of prospects, but you'll need to calculate the number of prospects you need to create the income you want. You'll be determining your conversion rate and tweaking your offer to reach the optimal response.

3.   You'll begin to craft your offer based on the needs of the prospects and the problems your product will solve. Make your offer based on the price and value of the product. If you have a low price, product, you could attract your market with a one-close sales letter. If your product is expensive, you might need to set up a series of closes to bring your prospects around. That means capturing your prospect's interest with a series of email tutorials on tackling their issues. Set up a series of closes to gain their trust and acceptance.

4.   Your website should have a special form to capture the name and email address of the prospects that come to your website. Once they sign up to receive more free information, you can continue to educate them on the benefits of your product. You can even continue to communicate with them regarding other associated products as long as you offer useful information on a regular basis.

5.   Use weekly email alerts, electronic press releases, joint venture email lists, e-zines, your personal blog and articles to develop organic search engine traffic. If you want to get from zero to sixty fast, use pay per click advertising to boost your traffic. Be sure to offer free information in your Pay Per Click ad.

This has been the fastest way to attract attention and generate your list. Don't forget the power of print. Use small local newspapers and Yellow Pages ads to gather more targeted prospects. Be sure to craft your ad with a free offer and send them to your website in order to fulfill the free offer.

6.   Get connected to other buyers and sellers in your product range. Offer incentives for them to carry your product or recommend your product to the people on their lists. Make it a point to test your ads regularly and track your progress.

7.   Work to systematize your online business. Regardless of your product, keep track of your clients and prospects, communicate with them regularly and you will succeed.

That should get you started in your planning phase. Get this down on computer or on paper so that you can assess some numbers. What will it cost you per lead; and how much will you need to make per customer to cover your costs and make a profit? These are the questions that will need firm answers.

Identify your real potential customers and separate them from the herd.

You will need to know what the ideal customer wants and how many of them are out there. Google and Yahoo will definitely help in spotting the exact profile. You can also go to forums in your niche and social network sites that feature your interests.

There is another aspect of marketing that you must be aware of - called psychographics. This relates to the unseen needs, wants, and desires of your market. If you are going to be in marketing and sales, you need to memorize this list. Here is Maslow's hierarchy of needs:

The base level houses the Physiological needs: Breathing, food, water, sex, sleep, homeostasis, and excretion. These needs must be met for normal biological functions. You can see why they are powerful motivators.

The second level houses the Safety needs: Security of body, of employment, of resources, of morality, of the family, of health, of property.

The third level houses the Love/Belonging needs: The need for friendship, family, sexual intimacy.

The fourth level houses the Esteem needs: Self-esteem, confidence, achievement, respect of others, and respect of others.

The fifth and highest level houses the need for Self-actualization: Morality, creativity, spontaneity, problem solving, lack of prejudice, acceptance of facts.

So why is this important in choosing a product and marketing it? Because smart entrepreneurs never make a product without first finding a need, want or desire to fill.

The greatest business people look for a problem in search of a solution. What Abraham Maslow gave marketers was a shorthand profile of needs, wants and desires and the framework for advertising products.

World famous author, performance coach and motivator Anthony Robbins promotes another compelling set of human priorities which he calls the Six Human Needs. These are:

* Certainty

* Variety

* Significance

* Connection or Love

* Growth

* Contribution

Keep these principles in mind when communicating with your target audience, and attempt to draw the right conclusions regarding their issues. Remember that people are interested in creating solutions to their situation not in buying things.

A solid gold Rolex is not just a watch, it represents something much more significant. When choosing a product, take into account where your target market falls in the hierarchy. Where do your ideal customers fall in the needs level?

Take a look at the problems your target market faces and match them to the levels on the list. Once you're able to identify the needs of your target market, with the problems your products solve, you'll be able sell to the right people and generate massive income.

Bring in 5,000 targeted prospects to your site in 30 days

So if you have no subscribers at this time and you want to make a decent entry level income in your online business what will you need to do? I'm going to return to the venerable Anthony Robbins again and refer to his principle of RPM. RPM refers to RESULT, PURPOSE, and MASSIVE ACTION.

I'm a stickler about this, but that's because I feel that anything less than 5,000 subscriber list can disappear in a heartbeat. People are fickle, and just like statistics; you will not be able to get much accuracy in your sampling with a much smaller list.

Let's say you want to be able to replace your $3,500 a month job and you figures that you have five products - a free product for $0.00, an eBook for $10.00, an application for $50.00 a training program for $100.00 and a complete online coaching system for $500.00.

Before you begin selling your $500.00 program you build a strong list of subscribers with your free eBook. You sell the $10.00 product in your OTO (One Time Offer). You now have customers coming from your OTO.

As you develop your relationship with your customers, you sell 60% of them your $50.00 program. As you develop a trust with your $50.00 customers, you find that 50% of them are ready for your $100.00 training program. As they become more familiar with your communication and support, 25% - 50% of those customers purchase your $500.00 package.

There are only three ways to get traffic to your site.

Everything you do will fall into:

Buying Traffic – Pay Per Click, Banner Ads, list rentals, E-zine ads etc.

Creating Traffic – Submission of articles, videos, press releases, social networking, tele-conferences, webinars etc.

Borrowing Traffic – Joint ventures, advertising swops, blog backlinks, etc. You can do a lot of horse trading if you work the forums.

So there you see the strategies of creating massive action if you build the plan around a clear set of goals.

Make compelling sales offers and killer e-mails that your leads really want

You may have been working on building your list for a while and haven't really gotten the results you've been hoping for. Here's a quick rundown on seven key areas to focus on when building your list of prospects. You may be doing some of them, but need to consolidate your strategy and like a good chef, combine your ingredients in the right proportion for maximum effect.

1) Use a fly trap.

That means you need to offer an incentive to your prospects that they would be interested in. If you don't have a free offer that matches the keywords that your ads or articles are optimized for, go out and get one. No one really wants a free book on candle making if they are looking for weight loss products.

2) Email strategy.

Know your numbers. First of all, know how many emails you need to have to make the kind of money you need. What market are you going to pursue? How many people can you get each day into your auto-responder and what kind of conversion will you need to have to make sales?

Suppose you figure that you need 25 to 50 subscribers a day to make the kind of money you want? How are you going to get them? What steps do you need to take to put that kind of traffic in your auto-responder on a consistent basis?

3) Article marketing.

If you have the time and the ability to create articles you can build a very big list. The issue is of course time and talent. It will take a bit of time to generate the necessary amount of optimized articles and then it will take a bit of time to build momentum.

4) Submit your articles to the top article directories.

Maintain consistently in production on your blog or Squidoo lens. You will need to stay consistent for the duration of the time it takes to reach critical mass. If you need to get to 5,000 subscribers on your list, you need to divide your critical mass number by the number of days you think you'll need to get there. What you are left with is the goal of attracting a certain amount of targeted subscribers by a certain date.

5) Understanding of your niche market.

You must first of all give some serious thinking as to which niche market, you intend to step into. Do the necessary research and continue to bolster that research to ensure that you know where to find the targeted enthusiasts who want your products.

6) Evaluate your systems.

If you get 4 to 5 new subscribers a day from article marketing, you must evaluate your tactics to get the rest of your daily supply of subscribers. If you need 25 subscribers a day and you are only getting 5, you now need to figure where the rest will come from.

7) Your blog

You might be able to get another 4 to 5 subscribers a day from your blog. Get a blog together that targets our niche. You will have to take time to make and maintain the blog though. The process takes time and work, I know. If you can tie your blog to Google Adwords and pump up your readership, you'll be able to add more people each day to your subscriber list.

Another reason to have a blog is to send regular updates to your list. It is not a good idea to bombard your list with offers every day, but you can set up a 30 day free training program by email and then a daily blog alert when your training program runs out. You can set up all that up in your auto-responder.

Start making sales with your existing customer list - no matter how small.

You've heard of viral marketing before, but have you ever thought of using it for your own business?

First, get in touch with several companies that offer great premiums. They need to be top-notch gifts that will get your client's attention. For example, there are companies that offer free vacation packages and free hotel packages. All you need to do is purchase these in bulk at super low rates. There are others that offer discounted high quality restaurant gift certificates and now I think you get the idea.

The offer has to be tangible; this item should be delivered in the mail or in person. The idea is to offer your existing clients an ethical bribe that will be passed on to their contact list. They will be offering the premium to members of their list on your behalf.

The offer is set up on a squeeze page and is a forced opt-in format. That means in order to get to the prize; the viewer has to enter their valid first name, email address, company name, phone number and the name of the person who recommended them. This last one is very important.

You want the referee to be honored with a prize of their own. You may not give them the same deal, it might be even better. The goal of the premium giveaway is to quickly develop a prospect list of warm leads from your client list.

When the new prospects get their gifts in the mail, you want to be able to let them know that they are going to be getting a call or email from you with another special offer.

You can offer them the same deal you offered to your clients; if they provide their contacts with a special offer, they can claim the benefits as well. If their contacts leave the name of their referrer in the online form, they will get a special bonus.

To implement viral marketing at your business; first, start with your customers. After you reach them, go to your suppliers; contact your friends and colleagues. The viral nature of the offer will bring a steady stream of prospects to your auto-responder. Be sure to put all your new prospects on an email newsletter or ezine to communicate with them regularly.

When picking a premium for your gift, pick something that everyone can enjoy. Try to stay away from controversial gifts offers. If you need more information, help in marketing ideas, or setting up your web-marketing program, let me know. Contact me for more details.

What to say to your new leads that will get them wanting what you have.

Remember when I mentioned the six human needs earlier? When you put your email campaign together, you will need to address the needs of your market. Your first email of course will be a welcome and a gracious explanation of who you are and what you do. The free gift you give your leads is a thank-you for the trust they had in you for the moment.

I would suggest you set up between 20 and 30 emails in your auto-responder to build an automatic follow up system. This system allows you to build a communications channel with your leads to maintain contact and to build confidence. Your goal is to move your leads through the sales funnel from prospects to customers and from customers to long term clients.

Do not try to sell your products to your leads in your introductory email. Establish a system of three to one in regards to sales offers. Give pertinent information that relates to the reason they came to you in the first place. You'll want to be the one they go to when they have questions regarding your specialty.

Throughout the series of emails, take your prospect through a series of steps that teaches them about the subject and also prompts them to give you answers regarding their needs. From time to time you'll want to get them to address those needs. Once they tell you what they really want, sell it to them.

Generate an automatic referral system to double your list in 30 days.

We covered the ideas of joint ventures in leads generation and getting your existing customers to refer others to your squeeze page. Let's put that to use again in jacking your list up to the 5k mark.

First, we need to establish that the rapport is there to make the referral system work; that means you don't want to get them moving on referrals until they buy something. Your leads are less likely to give you a referral because they don't know you.

Your customers will do it if you ask them to, and give them reasons to make the referral. Give them a picture of a positive outcome to their decision. Let them know that they are doing their contacts a favor.

Don't ask them to refer just anybody, give them the profile of the people that you are interested in helping. The reason that you are going to be particular in your selection is because you want to ensure that the recipient is qualified for your product or service.

Leave your customer with the impression that you are discriminating in your selection and not just fishing for a bunch of names. You can effectively boost your email list with warm prospects. Put your referral system on auto-pilot.

Build a system of perpetual online income with surveys.

The natural progression once you begin to work this system is to build your future products and services with the help of our growing team of marketing specials. Your customers should be the first group that you poll. It is better to phrase your surveys as a need for help or assistance.

Don't try to lead them to your conclusion. The best products will come from them, not from your assumptions. The goal should be to produce for the market. If you are successful at getting your customers to participate, you can continue to create highly marketable content for people that want what you need.

Don't get ahead of yourself by getting too confident. Grow your market and be patient with your customers. You can engage them far more liberally than your prospects because they tend to be more engaged.

Compose a different set of questions to your prospects or conduct spit tests on offers to analyze campaigns. This process allows you to continue to perfect your products as well as your marketing.

By removing the pressure to buy from your prospects, you begin to earn their trust and give them what they want. The great thing about this system is that you can put 90% of it on auto-pilot.

The wrap up:

Establishing an email marketing campaign takes time and focus. Set up your campaign with the audience in mind and be prepared to give them lots of useful information relating to their interests. You can sell to them but be mindful of spamming.

Double My Revenues In 12 Months Or Less

Successfully Market Anything

Marketing is the most important thing you can do in business after developing a great and indispensable product or service. Marketing will be one of your major initial expenses in many cases if you're a service oriented business. If you produce a product, it will be a close second.

Many people don't understand the value of marketing and consider it an afterthought that's why they end up with sleepless nights worrying about slow periods, lack of sales and rising competition later on. They were not educated in the basic principles of marketing. What I'm about to show you is the basic formula for selling your product or service.

If you don't have enough customers to cover your expenses, you're not effectively marketing your business. If your business is over five years old and you don't have a customer list that you communicate with each month, you're not marketing effectively.

So here is a simple five step formula for effective marketing:

1. Identify

Figure out the intended market for your product. Identify the ideal customer in as detailed a description as possible. What do they read? What products or services, do they buy that are related to your own?

2. Qualify

Your advertising will not promote your product or service. Your ad will focus on the most pressing problems that your service or product solves. The objective of your qualification advertising is to bring in qualified leads. The point of marketing is to find the prospects that need what you have or are willing to be persuaded to listen to what you have to offer.

3. Verify

You now verify your leads by making an offer. You make your pitch to the problems and or benefits that your prospects will think are important. If a prospect sees that the rewards are greater than the risks associated with commitment, they will buy. If they don't, you need to move them into the next step.

4. Edify

If the prospect has not purchased your products after the closing process, it's time to educate them on a consistent basis. Teach them about the issues surrounding their issues and problems (those associated with your product or service, of course.). You can offer free information and surveys to these prospects to keep them acquainted with your brand. Send them your newsletter.

5. Multiply

As you build a list of customers, you'll continue to build a growing list of prospects. As you continue to add more customers, you'll need to add more related products and services. The beauty of the process is that it will be much easier to sell new products to your customer list than to your prospect list. Just keep the processes going.

Make yourself "Google-able". That means if someone hears about you and looks you up online, they should find you on the first page. Whether it's your name, your business, your niche, you should be found on the first page on Google somehow. Obviously, if your name is John Smith, that is very difficult to find you, but if your name was John Dingleberry Smith, you'll have it made in the search engines.

Keep your promises and work on PR constantly in order to build your "web cred". The best practice for public relations you can perform on a regular basis is gathering testimonials from your satisfied clients. Get written, video and audio testimonials for the maximum credibility you want for your business.

Display your testimonials on your website or in your sales pages and emails. You can propose a trade for your testimonials; let your clients know that you will put a link from their website to yours. The legendary Dr. Joe Vitale has made it his mission to be a professional testimonials guy. He's on everything! The man is a ubiquitous endorser; you can be too. You will convert more prospects with the help of others because they bring social justification as well as enhancing your image.

So that is how you can effectively build a list of 5,000 subscribers while converting 60% sales over the next 30 to 60 days. Get out there and do it.

Useful Tools

Aweber.com

This is the auto-responder that I use. You can create auto-responder lists and track them. The service is used by most of the top marketers and companies on the Internet. The cost is very minimal and the legal protection is priceless.

ArticleMarketer.com

This is a premier service for distributing your articles to hundreds of article sites.

EzineArticles.com

My preferred website for publishing my articles. The submission is free with membership and you can track your readership.

The "Over the Hill" list

As you grow your list, begin to create subsets based on the length of time your subscribers have been registered. Studies have shown that there is a falloff of interest at around three months. You'll want to keep your older list members excited by acknowledging their longevity with special offers and or dynamic new material just for them.

One owner of a membership website elevates his older members to a more exclusive position every six months. He created a bronze, silver, gold, platinum and diamond membership position for his website. It might seem like a lot of work for maintaining a list of names, but that list is your lifeline and profit center. Regardless of the business you're in, a contact list of clients, prospects, vendors and mentors is the most important generator of business you'll come across, if you use it properly.

Keeping list members interested

If you've had a growing list spanning several years, you'll want to check your response rate as well as your click-through rate on special offers for older members of your list. Direct your older members to specially designed pages in your emails and track the response. See who clicks and responds to your test offers and who has not. Make it a point to test your list segments constantly.

Getting your emails noticed

When creating your e-mail messages, the two styles of delivery are important to distinguish. Some e-promoters prefer to deliver a complete message in the e-mail; others prefer to use a short introduction and a link to the main material on their website. Choose the method that suits your audience and your medium.

If you deliver multimedia information, a link to the source material is the preferred method, but you may want to use the two step method to test your audience response by tracking clicks to your squeeze page regardless of the message.

Double My Revenues In 12 Months Or Less

If you send out a regular newsletter and you prefer to give your reader the full story immediately, then you'll want to stick with the full e-mail letter format. This is especially important if you carry advertising at the bottom or in the body of your e-newsletter. It also ensures that your message is not overlooked or put off for another time. Some people will wait until later to click on the link to get to your message.

Your Subject line needs to be noticed

Your information still needs to be read regardless of the quality and the importance of the message. That means you need to get your e-mail noticed. Now you must think like an advertising agency. The subject line will be the most important part of your communication. Be sure to take the time to craft it for maximum punch and visibility. Think of the headlines you read in the paper and which ones grab your attention.

Which stories do you read after scanning the headlines? Your subject line should be as strong and compelling as those you find interesting. Be sure to include your company name and other identifying information in your subject line to alert your reader to whom you are. This lets them know that you are not a spammer or a stranger.

Create your message in dual format.

You might be one of the people who view the preview pane in your email browser; sometimes you quickly glance at the information and move on if it doesn't catch your interest. If what you see is a picture and that picture doesn't grab your interest, you're likely to move on as well.

When you build your e-mail, build it like a newspaper. The newspaper format has stood the test of time. If you create the top third of your e-mail message with the most important information, you will be able to persuade your reader to continue through to the end.

Build your message in both html and text format. The dual format will allow those with small format or "old school" e-mail tastes the style of reading they prefer. Those who prefer the graphic look of html can view it in their browser.

Using graphics to enhance the message

Using the newspaper format allows you to add images to enhance the text while allowing the text only browsers to fully understand the message without diluting its quality.

Keep the graphics simple and the file sizes small. The purpose of the graphics is to complement the copy. Because many people turn off their images in their e-mail browser, be sure to use ALT text in your html to indicate the titles of your graphics.

So how do you make a lot of money using e-mail?

Start with the list. Depending on the type of business you own, you can develop your list through an offer, you promote on the web or in print. If you can give something away, you will attract people to your offer.

If you use the Internet to generate leads, you can create articles geared to your market; distribute them to e-zines, blogs, and article sites. Place your blurb and a link at the bottom of your article that leads the reader to your website squeeze page (a special page dedicated to your marketing project on your website.).

Once you have your article and you promote it online through the above sources, the right readers who are attracted to your offer will give you their name and e-mail address in return for your offer.

Once you've collected your fresh hot list of interested prospects, begin to market to them by teaching them about your products or services. Establish the value and integrity up front, and you'll be able to keep them moving along the marketing channels. Consistent and worthwhile communication, build relationships; that makes for easier selling and massive profits.

The wrap up:

Your list is the biggest asset you have. Be sure to take a realistic attitude to email marketing. For some businesses, 300 people on their list might be enough. For most businesses, that won't even be a test case. Continue to communicate to your list at least once a month or in some cases once a week.

Getting Exposure

Getting noticed for the right reasons is called public relations.

Keep your strategic objectives in mind with any PR program that you initiate.

First, I recommend a Unique Slogan. You've seen enough commercials on TV to trigger the right response when I say "Coke is It." or "Fair and balanced". Companies spend millions to get their unique slogan into the minds of the public.

The unique slogan can be found in your mission statement or unique selling proposition. That's the quick summation of your company's marketing strategy. It's the focus of the company that separates from all other competitors or your answer to the problems of the marketplace you serve. I call it your Unique Slogan because in this modern age of sound bites, your message needs to be as short as possible.

What's your Unique Slogan?

Does it fit into a sound bite? Everyone talks about sound bites in a negative way. Sound bites are what we remember long after the message has been delivered. The key is to make your unique slogan - your sound bites memorable and meaningful.

Let's build your Unique Slogan.

Double My Revenues In 12 Months Or Less

What does your company stand for?

Are you an expert?

What is the most dominant feature that your company should be known for?

What's your hook? Your hook is the attention getting device or phrase that gets everyone to read past the headline.

What is the greatest benefit that your company offers its clients?

Once you have a firm grasp of your Unique Slogan you should be able to put it on your business card, email, and repeat it in your speaking engagements. This is what your company will be known for.

Build your PR toolkit

First, establish your contact database. You should have a list of media contacts both local as well as national. Your contacts should include web, print, radio and television. Your objective is to establish yourself as an expert. Your list should also include local business contacts as well as organizations. The media may or may not take you seriously, but don't worry about it.

More than anything else, you simply need to be consistent. Send out your press release once a month to the same sources. Set up a calendar of PR topics and stick to it. If possible, add more sources to the list and ensure the viability of your local list by contacting them by phone if you can.

The first few PR pieces will likely get tossed in the "round file" but after a few months, you'll soon discover that your press release will begin to show up. This is because your name will begin to gain familiarity.

You should also send your press releases to the online PR websites for mass distribution and to online news agencies. Include the contents of your press release in your monthly newsletter. That allows you to push yourself to find the newsworthy elements in your business. Your clients should receive this information regularly.

One of our favorite contributors, David Meerman Scott has contributed a special free book on the New Rules of Public Relations.

Go to http://www.awarenessnetworks.com to download his free e-book.

So what is a Public Relations and why is it so important?

Public relations help build awareness of companies, products, services, technologies, people and issues among key audiences and influencers. It helps companies create an identity in the industry, media and community.

Public relations is the use of editorial outlets (magazines, newspapers, broadcast), special events, newsletters and other PR tools to convey a message to a targeted audience. The fact is that public relations techniques are a discipline of management much like finance, accounting, human resources and law. There is a basic methodology that includes five points: goals, objectives, strategy, tactics and target audience.

What are the Tools of Public Relations?

There are many ways to reach target audiences. They are:

- News releases
- Public service announcements
- Guest editorials
- Media tours
- Broadcast/print interviews
- Photos/captions
- Video news releases
- Special events
- Sponsorships/contributions
- Press meetings
- Speaking opportunities
- bylined articles
- Other innovative avenues

What Can Public Relations do?

Public relations can add credibility/authority, create an opportunity to probe new markets for your product/service less expensive than advertising, test demand for new products in current markets and establish or increase awareness of your organization's message among key buyer and influence audiences.

What Can't Public Relations do?

With public relations your control of the message is more limited than with advertising. There is no guarantee of frequency, how often or how many times your message will appear, or placement, where your message will appear. With public relations a reporter/editor is being "sold" a story.

Even if the reporter "buys" the story, there is no guarantee of how or when he will use the story. However, PR has the advantage of third-party credibility. People tend to believe what they read much more than the ads they see. In fact, studies show that a reader is seven times more likely to respond to PR than to advertise and that article written by reporters are four times more believable than advertisements.

Establish your connections

Contact the people on your list at least once a month. You want to be available for comments or advice when the need arises. You will be amazed how many referrals you will generate from your PR contact list over time.

Implement a PR Strategy in 7 Days

Building publicity for you and your business can be done one day at a time.

Here's how to generate publicity for you and your business by spending just a little of each of the next seven days on PR:

Day 1: Determine your target.

Make a list of all the publications in your target market area. These will most likely be newspapers, such as weekly newspapers, daily newspapers, regional business journals, free about-town advertising fliers and chamber of commerce newsletters. Next, determine the radio and television stations in your target market area. This includes AM, FM, public radio, college radio stations and the like.

Day 2: Develop a database of contacts from day one.

From each of the publications, determine where your news or announcement would best fit. Once you have done this, find out who the primary editor or reporter is for this part of the publication. Sometimes this is a feature editor, a feature reporter, a pool reporter or the managing editor. Do not send your press release to anybody and everybody at a particular publication. Do the same thing for radio and TV producers: Find out who assigns the news to reporters. Find out who edits the on-air news.

Day 3: Determine what PR story you will communicate.

Brainstorm PR topics. Are you making an announcement, communicating a change, stating an opinion or revealing a finding? Do you have a local angle to a national story? Is your information newsworthy and not promotional slanted? All you need is 12 topics to average one press release per month for one year. However, don't let this schedule stop you from reporting news when it happens or making an announcement.

Day 4: Write the actual press release.

Editors love people who speak their language. A one-page press release that opens with who, what, where, when and why will make them happy and increase your probability of getting into their publication. Include some background information, a quote from you or another high-ranking person in the organization and the contact information. That's all there is to a press release. It doesn't have to be a long thesis. It doesn't have to have every single detail in it. If the reporter wants to do more of a story, he or she will call to develop further.

Day 5: Send your press release to those in the database, you established on day two.

Some editors prefer faxed press releases, yet there is a growing trend toward receiving them by e-mail. Very rarely are press releases snail-mailed; however, some still are when photos are part of the release. Finding out your editor's, reporter's or producer's preference will increase your chance of publicity.

Day 6: Use your press release for other things.

Because of the sheer number of press releases generated, they cannot all be published. Don't let this stop you from issuing the release and trying to generate publicity. There are other things you can do with press releases. You can post them on your Web site in the media room area.

You can use them as direct-mail pieces to customers and prospects. You can use them as handouts on sales calls or put them on the other side of your fliers. Use your imagination here, and you will be surprised at the unique ways you have to generate publicity and ultimately buzz about you and your business.

Day 7: Continue your efforts to establish relationships with editors, reporters and producers.

The more relationships you have with your targeted publications, the increased likelihood you have of getting publicity. The time to do this is not when you have a breaking news story. Take your time in this area and spread out your efforts. Then when you do have that breaking news or blockbuster story, you'll know who to contact directly and quickly for the biggest PR impact.

Spending just a little bit of time each day on these seven steps will make you an expert in the PR arena. The most appealing part of all about this kind of PR strategy is the cost. In the spirit of guerrilla marketing, this is not high-dollar marketing, but rather marketing that relies on your time, energy and imagination.

The proper use of newsletters and email
Your PR mailing should be purely informational. You're selling your company's expertise in problem solving. The people who you will mail or email regularly will be reminded of you, but not bothered by you. The idea of writing regularly may scare you if you don't do it regularly, but there are many online places to obtain content. You then add your own personal material to the content to fill it out.

You will be building your brand and reputation throughout this phase.

Set up speaking engagements, if you really want to get massive exposure to promote your business. Join local organizations and write. Become a guest columnist or blogger for your local newspaper or its online edition.

Getting noticed for the right reasons is priceless for generating the kind of image that leads to more sales leads.

You can get up to speed quickly by going to www.pressreleasehelp.com for mass press release distribution on the web.

Other sources for online public relations distribution and press release assistance are:

PRWeb.com

PR Newswire.com

Massmediadistribution.com

I-newswire.com

Prlog.com

101PublicRelations.com

PR Alone isn't enough.

To make the most of your marketing strategy, reach out to prospects in more ways than one.

Just getting your company's name printed in the paper will not lead to numerous phone calls from interested prospects. PR is not a marketing cure-all. How often do you call someone or call a company because you saw them mentioned in a newspaper or magazine article? Chances are; you've done it very few times-if ever. That's because mentions in the press, appearances on radio and TV, and other PR are just more "touches" in the world of marketing.

Marketing is made up of many things that all work together. It's an integrated approach that combines a variety of strategies, tactics and weapons. PR represents just one of these.

Now, put that newspaper mention or TV/radio appearance together with an advertisement, a direct sales call, an encounter at a networking event, a postcard in the mail, a public presentation or a drive by your business location, and something will happen. Your phone will ring. Prospects will come to you. Your business will increase.

It is generally said that it takes six to eight times to get your name, service, brand or product to the point of achieving top-of-mind awareness with your prospects and customers. One PR touch combined with all the other touches mentioned above, generally achieves this top-of-mind awareness. Your company, product or service will be at the top of a prospect's mind when it comes time for her to purchase your product or service.

Even though I stated that marketing is made up of many things, these things are really just "hits." The six to eight hits; can be six to eight of the same things.

They can be six to eight mention in the newspapers, six to eight appearances on TV or six to eight times people see you at a networking event. Usually, concentrated efforts like these take time, which is why the assortment approach works best. With the assortment approach, that one mention can then turn into a phone call, a visit or an order.

The assortment approach is needed to supplement your PR because PR:

• Can't tell the whole story.

• Doesn't sell.

• Doesn't always provide the necessary contact information for readers and viewers.

PR is generally news-related. The news isn't a sales pitch; news is information for interested prospects. This information then needs to be processed, filtered and fertilized by other touches and other marketing to grow into fruit-bearing sales or calls.

PR is not an event as many business owners believe. It is just one component of the whole marketing process. Constantly managing the process will keep your marketing from being events.

Because not every press release issued by you will generate placement or broadcasts, just getting that one mention or viewing is still a challenge. Consistent, frequent and persistent communication with the media increases the probability of appearances on an ongoing basis, which increases sales and profits. So don't stop going after that mention, regardless of how many times it takes.

For most businesses, the New Year is a time for assessment, goal setting and strategic planning. When it comes to PR, this is the time to set objectives and formulate a clear, defined plan that'll help your business achieve optimum results in the media.

When planning your PR activities for the year, as a general rule, consider the full year ahead, plan for six months, and expect to revise after three months. Like most business activities, PR requires flexibility and a recognition that things will change over time. However, there are a number of factors that'll make a measurable difference to your company's success if you take them into account at this early stage.

Assess & Plan

First, review the past year in terms of PR activity. If your business received media attention last year, review the resulting coverage with an analytical eye. Determine the angles and pitches that worked well and resulted in positive coverage.

Take note of which journalists reported in your favor and which didn't. Look at the overall amount of positive, negative or neutral coverage you received. If you subscribed to a media measurement service, assess the results of your campaigns and, if possible, compare your progress against your competitors.

Next, consider your overall business objectives, and use these as a basis for developing your key media messages. Make sure that what you say and how you say it reflects what you're trying to achieve. Your messages will form the backbone of your communication activity for the year.

Finally, develop a plan of attack. Review your business plan through the eyes of a journalist - what would be of interest to your customers or investors?

Identify potential media opportunities that could occur during the year, such as product launches, expansion activities and new service offerings, and develop a calendar that lists the events. If you can, try to organize major news events to create the most buzz. For instance, if your company is introducing a new line of beach apparel, time the launch in the spring to coincide with warming temperatures.

Always remember to put your goals and objectives in writing so you can refer back to them throughout the year and evaluate your success.

Tools & Tactics

Once you've sketched out your plans for the year, it's time to consider the activities that'll enable you to achieve your objectives.

• Establish a news release calendar to plan out the news releases you intend to issue throughout the year. You may need to revise this calendar as you move through the year, but it'll give you some initial structure to adhere to and help you stay focused on generating news.

• Media outreach in the form of pitching reporters and placing articles is still the essence of PR, and the foundation for any PR program is a solid media list. Before engaging in any PR activities, take the time to carefully research and build a database of key reporters. Your list should contain the contact details of the publications and journalists that pertain to your industry and be organized according to how valuable each is in terms of reaching your target audience.

Once you've created a list, schedule time on your calendar for media outreach. Contact each reporter individually to introduce yourself and to arrange informal meetings where you can discuss the outlook for your company and industry.

• Publications' editorial calendars offer an excellent vehicle for planning media exposure. Researching them will enable you to identify opportunities to offer yourself as an expert source, contribute an article or even suggest a feature on your company. Once you've set your list of targets, begin contacting them as soon as possible. Most editorial outlets have deadlines several months ahead of their publication dates. Pay careful attention to the closing dates, or you'll risk losing out on the opportunity.

• Contributed or "blind" articles can be an excellent way to generate exposure and establish you as an industry expert. Research magazines, newspapers and websites to find those outlets that are open to such articles, then contact the editor to propose a topic.

Remember to make sure the focus of the media outlet is in sync with your business objectives and the article contains your key messages.

• Case studies are very attractive to the media because they offer a tangible, real-world example of the benefits of your product or service.

The challenge with developing case studies is they require active customer participation.

So talk to your clients and ask them if you can report on their successes. While this'll require your customers to share their "war stories," it offers them--and you--a chance to shine.

• Speaking opportunities offer another avenue for generating exposure. When planning your PR activities for the year, research conferences, trade shows and webinars for opportunities to nominate yourself as a keynote speaker or a member of a panel discussion.

The value in securing such engagements can be tremendous, especially for a growing business; however, they also require vigilant planning because most speaking opportunities are finalized several months in advance.

• Blogs and social media have grown in popularity as communications tools because they offer a way to have an active discussion with a motivated audience.

When considering PR tactics, don't forget to research the blogs that relate to your industry and get to know the styles and personalities of their authors. Technorati, the leading blog search engine, is a great place to start.

A presence in the blogosphere can add to your company's perception as a thought leader. But remember, all material published on a blog is open to a wide audience and can initiate a line of discussion that may not always jive with your point of view.

If you want to launch your own blog, there are free tools, such as Blogger and Blog.com that enable you to do this easily. When it's all set up, make sure it gets listed on Technorati.

The Internet also contains a number of social media networks such as del.icio.us and Digg. These networks are used to store and share content and information--like articles--among members.

Additionally, if you have video content that you'd like to share with a consumer audience, you should familiarize yourself with video sharing sites such as YouTube and Metacafe.

• Crisis planning is also an essential part of your business's PR plan. This should include all possible negative scenarios and the appropriate responses to them. Ensure that other members of your business are aware of crisis procedures, and take time to do a test run to help iron out any inconsistencies or holes in your plan.

Planning your PR strategy now will not only help generate new ideas and opportunities for you and your business to shine, it'll give you peace of mind in your day-to-day operations. While PR plans are always subject to change, planning ahead will enable you to stick to your overall goals and maintain your focus.

You should not underestimate the power of a book on your specific products or service. Your book gives your company credibility. You are now the definitive expert.

The wrap up:

If you need to remember anything about the strategies of Public Relations it's this; establish a Unique Slogan; make a full 6 to 12 month plan with all the important information on your company. Establish a relationship with local media outlets.

Customer Retention Systems

"It's cheaper to keep 'em."

By all accounts, it now costs nine times more to get a new client, than it costs to keep an existing client coming back for more.

So, what is the secret to keeping clients coming back for more?

The Four Pillars of Customer Retention.

- o Great initial service.
- o Consistent follow-up procedures.
- o Continuing client education.
- o Ongoing personal touch.

Great Initial Service

Develop customer service standards and procedures. This will assure consistent quality of service even when things get really busy.

Establish Follow-up Procedures.

Develop a follow-up system that touches your clients at least once a month. If you have a newsletter or email alerts that go out regularly, keep it consistent for maximum effect.

Continuing Client Education.

Empower your clients with knowledge. By educating them about your product or service, you bind them to you. You become the expert who they can rely on for solving their problems relating to your field.

The Personal Touch.

Establishing a relationship binds your clients to you as well as you to your clients. That means the relationship cannot be one-sided. Establishing trust and a feeling of security is paramount when creating this bond. Trust and security creates loyalty.

Example of Customer Retention

Here's an example of the classic way to execute customer retention systems. A chiropractor keeps tabs on her patients with birthday cards and anniversary cards. She also sends out Mothers' Day and Fathers' Day cards and other holiday cards to select patients. She sends out email newsletters, monthly and mails out a few by snail mail.

Customer Retention Systems

She conducts a business health seminar twice a year and videotapes it for her website. She then makes it available on her website to anyone interested in workplace safety.

Patient Follow-up Procedures

Her staff has all patients entered in the customer relationship management (CRM) software and sends out alerts for follow-ups along with special offers for their friends and families.

Double My Revenues In 12 Months Or Less

Customer Relationship Systems (CRM) software can help you to develop controls for automating your processes. There are several top notch CRM software packages available depending on your price range-

Microsoft Dynamics CRM

Advantages of Microsoft Dynamics CRM 3.0 Software:

Microsoft Dynamics CRM is a customer relationship management (CRM) software used to create a clear picture of customers.

Its sales, marketing and customer service chapters deliver speed, flexibility and afford ability, drive measurable improvements, enhance relationships and increase profitability.

Pivotal CRM

Advantages of Pivotal CRM Software:

Now you can automate all facets of marketing, sales and customer service relationships between company employees, business partners and customers to manage all your valued business relationships for long-term growth and profit

e-Synergy

Advantages of e-Synergy Software:

The seven chapters of e-Synergy allows you to share HR data, accounts, documents, projects, logistical data, financial data and workflow. Communicate electronically with customers, resellers and suppliers through the portals.

GoldMine Enterprise Edition

Advantages of GoldMine Enterprise Edition Software:

GoldMine Enterprise Edition provides enterprise class CRM functionality with quick time to benefit and low total cost of ownership. GMEE can be tailored to make your users more productive, drive revenue, and provide better insight into your business.

The wrap up:

Start now to develop or fine-tune your client follow-up system. Like any good investment, it will appreciate over time, but you must be consistent in applying it.

Double Your Revenues

This is the point at which we look at the reason for all this talking.

What will it take to double your revenues?

The secret to economic success is in the systems you run. You've heard that before. Profitable systems will allow you to walk away, go on vacation and come back richer than when you left.

If you have a system for each phase of your business, you have a better chance for success than most businesses that don't. Here's the reality; unless it's a franchise, most companies don't have a set of systems that they follow and regularly evaluate. What marketing systems are you dedicated to using that are working for you? Look at the previous chapter to establish the optimum strategies for your type of business model.

First, please remember the rule – "If it ain't broke, don't fix it." What you need to do to double your income is first and foremost, identify your current income.

How much are you making each month?

Be fully aware of the process that you used to earn your current income. Evaluate the current strategies and identify what's working and what needs to go. What steps did it take to make it and how much is it costing you? Are you earning your company's income or do you have employees earning it for you?

Can you walk away for two weeks and confidently say that your business is running smoothly without you? If the answer is no, you need to check out your systems.

Review the systems you currently have.

Audit them for effectiveness. If you find that your marketing costs $30.00 for each new client, you now have a starting point to work with. You can start by reducing your cost per client or increasing the number of clients you get for your money.

Look at your marketing plan and determine if you are in the right business. I mean are you structuring your product or service to its maximum benefit? Examine your positioning within your market. Identify the real benefits and value to your market by conducting surveys and client reviews.

Next:

Decide if you need to:

- Improve the current systems.
- Optimize your current systems.
- Implement a new system.
- Test, Audit, and retest again.
- Add incremental improvements.

Doubling your revenues requires attention to detail. You'll take a serious look at what is working in your company and what is not. Begin to apply the strategies you learned in the other chapters and track them for effectiveness. Once you learn how to gage your progress, you'll know what to optimize, what to let go, what to streamline and what to invest more time and money in.

I know that the information I'm giving you is not sexy or exciting, but think of what you will be able to do with your life once you put your business on auto-pilot. You can add your own excitement and sexiness to your business once you've doubled your revenues and taken yourself out of the business' day to day activities and become free to run it instead.

The secret to economic success is in the systems you run.

An example might be a chiropractor who wants to increase her business by 50% in 6 months. She first establishes how many new patients she currently has and how many more she needs to fill her monthly quota in order to reach her goal.

Her business model's profile is - "service to consumer", so these are the optimal marketing strategies she uses:

Referrals-

Newspaper ads-

Incentives-

Coupons-

Circulars and fliers-

Yellow page ads-

Website-

Blog-

E-book-

Webinars-

Publicity-

She determines that in order to increase her revenues by 50% she needs to add 20 new patients a month. That's 5 new patients a week. Now our chiropractor determines that she has 380 patients that currently see her each year. After reviewing her past patient list, she can also contact an additional 160 past patients to re-connect with her practice.

She needs 260 new patients for the year to reach her goal based on her calculations of treatment and product sales. She also needs to review her current strategies to see what's working and what's working so-so.

Our chiropractor decides to concentrate on referrals, publicity and newspaper ads to generate the leads necessary for her growth.

Her newspaper ad announces an online promotion that teaches chronic back pain sufferers how to avoid injury and relieve their pain. People who are interested can go online to a special page and sign up to get the guide. She wants to collect a steady stream of interested potential patients that she can reach through email.

She sends a letter to all her current and past patients telling them about the online seminar that teaches chronic back pain sufferers how to cope. She offers an incentive to her current patients and former patients as well in the form of a free guide and a coupon.

As people go to the website, they enter their names and email addresses into the opt-in form; once they validate their submission, they are taken to a section of her website and view the series of online training and they leave the site and collect their free guide to overcoming back pain.

This leads to an offer to come in for an initial exam. She passes out the same information at her monthly networking group with an incentive to her fellow members to pass on that information to their friends and family.

Her website begins to populate its marketing database. She now has a base of subscribers to her series of online seminars. They also visit her blog and contribute questions to it. As more people read her online information, our chiropractor gains more credibility. The more contacts she has with her prospective patients, the greater the chance of them making an appointment and coming in for treatment.

Her contact database is used to capture the emails and allow her to send out regular information on health and fitness and pain management I the form of newsletters. This update also has incentives for coming in for an initial exam.

After several weeks of consistent promotion, she begins to see a small increase of new prospects and a return of old patients who had not been in to see her in years. She has now established a live monthly seminar for patients and offers an incentive for attending. The patients get an even better incentive for bringing a guest.

The seminars are videotaped and appear on her website and on YouTube. She now points her remaining prospects and patients to the videos for viewing.

Within three months, our chiropractor sees a flood of activity from old patients as well as referrals. She also sees new patients from the local promotions through her newsletters and seminars. With consistent tracking, our chiropractor is on track to succeed.

The wrap up:

If you need to remember anything about the strategies of marketing it's this; use the appropriate marketing strategies for your business model. Always test your systems and start simply and conservatively.

Once you have a system that works, slowly expand it and re-test it. Treat your marketing like wheat or corn in the field. Don't be impatient while it's growing, give it a chance. Once it sprouts, increase the activity. Continue to grow it properly to ensure consistent growth.

Double Referrals

One of the fastest ways to double your revenues is to tap into your existing network of clients. Your clients can be your best source of new business if you know how to approach the strategy of referral marketing.

You first must be sure that your existing policies have put you in a good relationship with your existing client base. Have you paid close enough attention to your existing clients?

Key questions to ask yourself about your current clients:

- What is the Lifetime Value of a client for your business?
- What is your initial income from an average client?
- What is the client repurchase rate?
- What is your average repurchase income?
- How long is your average client lifespan?
- Let's calculate an average Lifetime Value Example.

This is from our chiropractor's worksheet

Example: Initial fee = $75.00

+ ($33.5 revisit fees 8 a year x 4 years (lifespan)

=$1072.00 Lifetime Value

Our chiropractor has been in business for 10 years.

Average patient valued at $269.00 a year.

Patient LTV at $1072.00 each.

(Average patient = 4 years.)

Now that we know the average value of a client, we need to take a look at a system to cultivate more of them.

That means developing a referral system

1. Develop a policy – How will you handle referrals?

2. Create a letter or postcard and email template that will go to your associates, family and friends.

3. Incorporate your V.I.P. List and begin to organize a referral network.

4. Build a Referral Partnership Network.

5. Your current client list – implement your referral program within your follow up.

6. Employee Referral Program

When you develop your policy, be sure to maintain consistency in practice.

If you decide to send out a "thank you" card to any client who successfully refers a new one, do it EVERY TIME. If you generate referrals by inviting clients and their guests to an event, thank them when they bring a guest.

Take ONE idea and implement it.

Test it and be consistent for at least 3 months. Tweak it if there is even a minimal positive result. Success comes from consistent positive action on your ideas.

How can you develop a turn-key perpetual referral machine?

I've spoken with many small business owners over the years and they all want the same thing. They want unlimited referral business without taking the enormous amount of time needed for developing the referral base. There is not one small business owner who would not love to get 100% of the referrals their clients hand out. The problem is, very few businesses actually know how many times their clients have referred a friend or family to their company.

The referral strategies used by small business are inconsistent and usually impossible to track properly. I'm going to give you three strategies to consider for your business marketing. These will allow you to develop a record of your efforts and allow you to adjust to your unique circumstance.

1. It all starts with consistent customer service.

There should be a massive effort to develop a step-by-step program of above average service. Once you've created that program, offer it to every client, big or small. Use customer service surveys to uncover the needs of your market.

Before you contact past clients for the purpose of getting referrals, establish a warm up period. If you've been in touch with them regularly, there should be no problem making the pitch. Create a series of offers in the form of letters of emails. Create several letters. You'll want to create awareness in your clients that you do most of your business by referrals. Take them through your process and give them the tools to offer referrals to their friends and family.

A series of articles that point out the problems potential clients might have and how your type of service solves them can be mailed out or emailed to your existing clients as a way to spread the word. You can instruct your clients on the proper time and ways to distribute your information.

Your articles can be timely such as "10 ways to overcome.... Or "How to recognize the symptoms of..." These types of articles allow your clients to pass them on to their friends and family without the pressure. A series of these helpful articles will also work well in the local papers and on the Internet.

You can include an offer or point the reader to more information on your website.

You can generate referral business by offering a free seminar or tutorial along with an incentive for guests of your existing clients. The offer can be time sensitive in order to generate greater interest. (See our tools section for sample referral letters.)

2. Create a network of partners who share referrals.

Several business owners can work together to create a referral network of non-competing partners. The group can share referrals on a regular basis.

Another networking concept along the same lines is to prepare a professional referral form for your clients to fill out that lists the names of services they currently refer to others. Call their list of services and find out more about them. Let them know that you routinely refer your clients to trusted service providers and you want to know if they do the same. Depending on your client list, you can quickly develop a network of several hundred people.

3. Your testimonial collection is a goldmine.

Build a testimonial letter collection. Better yet, get your best clients on audio and video. This is a powerful endorsement to new clients and works well in connection with the above concepts.

You can build your business to the point where the majority of your business is powered by referral marketing; it takes time, systems and constant care and attention. Creating a suite of marketing systems for your business is a major undertaking. Maintaining the systems and consistently following it is even harder.

Creating Your Turn- Key Systems

Ten Essential Factors for Successful System Automation.

Creating a suite of marketing systems for your business is a major undertaking. Maintaining the systems and consistently following it is even harder. There are many turn-key systems out there that might be able to get you going, but the best turn-key systems must fit your most successful procedures and policies.

What if you could automate 90% of your systems so that one or two trained assistants could maintain them? Would you be more inclined to get it done and manage such a system? What if you could automate your marketing system to four hours of activities each month?

Before you can automate any system, you have to establish it first. The systems and procedures should be in operation for at least three months and established as viable and practical. Where do you begin to establish a huge undertaking such as this?

What do you look for in terms of computerized solutions? How much could something like this cost, and is it worth it? How detailed will your process be? Can you create the system with existing software and training?

Here are the ten essential factors for successful system automation:

1. You must have control of the system.

A buddy of mine had a tech guru in another country build a complete e-commerce, auto responder and membership management system and got it up and running for a pretty decent price. Eight months into the operation of the business, he had a major glitch in the affiliate management portion of the software and needed to have it fixed fast.

138

He not only could not get in touch with the programmer, he had no idea where the backup system for the database in which his affiliates and their payment history were stored. He had no idea where his server information was located. It was a wakeup call to keep control of his systems. He eventually got the problem taken care of but what a hiccup in a $12,000 a month business that turned out to be!

2. The system must follow a logical process.

3. The system must be easy to understand and implement.

4. Any Internet application must have an in-office backup.

5. Reports and tracking features should be easy to obtain and understand.

6. When planning the automated, secure technical help from experts.

7. Remember that your time is best spent growing your business.

8. Avoid expensive proprietary options-

9. Don't get stuck with outdated technology.

10. Do the calculation of the ROI to ensure that the system pays for itself.

Indispensable Resources for Success

There are several companies on the Internet that can set up a complete turn-key system for your company for both on and off-line sales and marketing. They cover a wide variety of options to handle various facets of business operation.

It's getting easier to find computerized solutions for small business needs. We will explore and review a few companies in the coming months to get an idea of their capabilities. If you have a special need and would like us to address it, let me know and we'll do some checking for you.

Here are some resources for you to research for your turnkey marketing:

List building

The quality of your lists will determine the success of your direct marketing campaign. 80% of your marketing battle is getting the right lists. The best source for mailing lists for rent is the SRDS at www.SRDS.com.

This is the directory of choice of the direct marketing industry. You really are not serious about marketing if you are not regularly using the SRDS List Book. You should also be able to find the SRDS List Book at your local library if you'd like to save the roughly $700 you would have to pay to subscribe to SRDS.

This is the single most valuable resource for anyone in the business of direct marketing . . . or, frankly, for just about anyone in business.

A good list company.

Melissa Data at www.MelissaData.com is one of the nation's largest list companies. The contact I work with is Ralph McFann. You can email him at ralph@melissadata.com. You'll want to enlist his help as you plan your next direct marketing campaign. You should be able to find just about any list you'll need for your marketing campaign by going through Melissa Data. And they'll help you avoid making costly list mistakes.

For commissioned sales people, take a look at www.SalesGenie.com. I've used them for generating sales leads for chiropractors and the list is pretty good. The parent company is www.InfoUSA.com which I have used successfully for many years in my Yellow Pages sales program.

Another recommendation is a company called Harris InfoSource. I haven't used them yet, but they come highly recommended. Here's the domain name, you can reach them at: http://www.harrisinfo.com/HarrisInfo/Home.aspx.

One of my mentors, Ben Hart recommends this company as well. www.wholesalelists.net

Target your niche

Writers Market at www.WritersMarket.com is a catalogue of thousands of specialty and niche publications (with their subscription and circulation numbers). Many of these publications will rent their list to you for a one-time use for your mailing. And all will sell you space ads.

Data mining.

There are many markets out there to tackle, but you could go broke chasing all of them. The best way to approach the area of lists is to narrow your focus.

Good data mining accelerates the process of finding where the money is on your list – whether current customers or prospects (this is key if you are selling financial services, consulting services, pricey real estate, vacations, cosmetic surgery, a recreational product or any kind of luxury or non-necessity of life).

A great List Broker is worth their weight in gold. List brokers are paid 20% commission. Their commission is built into the price of the list. There might be a minimum for small orders.

Writing and creative services

Graphic art, website design and copywriting. At www.eLance.com you'll find plenty of affordable talent to handle all your creative, design and writing needs. You can get a beautiful, fully functional and highly professional website for $300-$500. Many of the website designers you'll find here are from India, Eastern Europe and the developing world. These people are hungry and smart. www.craigslist.org is another place to put out bids for freelance work you need performed. This is the largest classified ad service on the Web.

Need a custom software application for your website or computer network? You'll find the solution at www.RentACoder.com; it works just like eLance. I use them a lot for website projects and database issues. You describe the job you want done and put it out for bid. Even when I have not needed custom code, I've also used RentACoder.com to assist me on program applications and found them to be very helpful.

You'll be asked to deposit a sum of money into an escrow account before bidding out a project. This is excellent protection for you and your vendor. Once the job is done, just authorize the payment. It's pretty easy.

I use www.1Shoppingcart.com as my shopping cart system. This third-party hosted solution includes many marketing tools needed by eMerchants -- including email broadcasting and auto responder service, ad tracking, customizable order forms and order buttons, affiliate tracking and easy integration with all the major merchant account and transaction gateways. www.quickpaypro.com is another shopping cart with lots of additional marketing bells and whistles -- including affiliate tracking software, etc. Definitely worth a look.

I also use OS Commerce when building shopping cart systems into websites. This open source shopping cart works well if you want to incorporate a shopping cart into your website for no monthly costs.

I use www.Authorize.net as my merchant account gateway. I'm very happy with it. Many of my associates use them as well. They also have recurring payment options for membership site payments.

For membership website payment systems, I use www.amember.com. They have a wide variety of plugins that allow you to protect areas of your website as well as secure payment solutions for your membership program.

You should also have a PayPal account -- www.PayPal.com. I personally find PayPal difficult to work with. They make merchants jump through too many hoops. But you will lose sales if you don't offer a pay-through-PayPal option. Some buyers feel more comfortable and secure paying through PayPal. The advantage of PayPal is that you don't need to have another merchant account or even a shopping cart. You can be up and running taking orders right away.

Yahoo provides start-up merchants one of the easiest, cheapest solutions for getting up and running fast. Just head on over to http://smallbusiness.yahoo.com. The transaction fee is a very low 1.5%. You can have a website, a shopping cart, a merchant account, even products to sell in minutes.

Another way to get started selling instantly on the Internet is with eBay Storefronts. Their website is similar to Yahoo's. You can get to their website at http://pages.ebay.com/storefronts/start.html.

eBay's merchant and storefront service has all the tools you need. They also have an extensive knowledge base. You can learn all about building a shop from their main website.

If your online business is a bit more complex and more advanced, www.NetSuites.com is a comprehensive e-commerce solution to take a look at. I haven't used them, but they are highly recommended.

Add Voice and Video to Your Websites

Click here to add audio to your website. Using audio in my internet marketing has increased my response rates by at least 500%.

Click here to add streaming video to your website and Internet marketing. Using video will help turn your website into a talking sales force that can deliver your sales presentations perfectly to thousands of people, even millions of people, at the same time.

To create audiovisual presentations on your website and develop fantastic tools

Add graphics to your site

Adobe PhotoShop and PaintShop Pro are certainly essential tools for producing quality graphics you can use Open Office for some graphics work as well as the open source product Paint.net. Another great open source paint product is Gimp. These free products rival their expensive cousins for ease of use, stability and power.

Fiverr.com is a great place to get quick services for a low price. You can get voice over talent, graphics and a whole lot more. Be careful because the quality may not always be great. Most services are $5.00 so you can be sure to get some great deals.

I've been producing graphics for most of my life, but not everyone wants to do that so thank God for the Internet. There's an almost unlimited supply of professional graphics (much of it free) that you can just grab off the Internet. Here are some sites to go to for free graphics:

www.addesigner.com

(Best tool I've found for designing animated banners)

www.windyweb.com

(Excellent collections of graphics, clip art)

http://www.angelfire.com

(Great collection of buttons and graphics for your site)

www.TemplateKingdom.com

(Great website templates. Just grab one and follow it)

www.ArtToday.com

(Photos and art)

www.pambytes.com

(Clip art, templates, and backgrounds)

www.clip-art.com

(Big data base of art and graphics)

www.free-backgrounds.com

(Backgrounds and borders)

www.pixelfoundry.com

(Backgrounds)

http://www.bigbeautifulbackgrounds.com/page1.htm   (Cosmic   and abstract backgrounds)

http://buttonland.com

(All kinds of buttons to use on your site)

To grab images off the Web, simply use the "Right Click" on your mouse and choose "Save Picture As." Then just follow the instructions of your Web editing software to put the images on your site.

Email marketing

Here are the email marketing systems I use: http://www.aweber.com or http://www.iContact.com.

Auto responders, Newsletters, and List Management.

Email is how you reach your opt-in subscribers with follow-up communications. Overall, I like Aweber. It's cheaper and has more functionality than iContact. Aweber is the best of the low-cost email marketing services.

But the downside of Aweber is that if someone buys your product but is not already on your email list in Aweber's system, Aweber will require them to verify that they want to get emails from you before you can put these buyers on your Aweber list.

The result: 25% will not verify that they want to hear from you. So you won't be able to communicate with 25% of your buyers (who are not already on your Aweber list). Not a good thing. What you'll have to do is give them an incentive to opt in.

I've also noticed that many of the Internet marketing gurus use Aweber while many of the public relations firms and ad online ad agencies use Icontact.

Toll-Free Phone Numbers

Add 1-800 toll-free numbers and "24-Hour Recorded Message Hotlines" to your marketing. This is much more than another toll-free 800 number service.

Here's a sophisticated marketing tool you probably don't know about that lets machines snag your leads and make your sales pitches for you, automatically.

Lower-Cost Toll-Free Phone Numbers can be found at www.TollFreeMax.com

Direct mail

Card Decks and Cooperative Mailings. This is a great way to share costs on your mailing with other merchants and businesses. Instead of your postcard costing 50 cents each if you mail it solo, you can mail your postcard in an ADVO card deck for as little as 2 cents each.

Use this tool for lead generation and build lists of very hot prospects. Click here for more on how to use card decks and co-op mailings. The leading vendors in this arena are www.ADVO.com, www.MoneyMailer.com and www.ValPak.com

These companies will give you great value for your investment.

Great mail shop for high-end direct mail.

RST Marketing is a highly personalized, high-end, high-impact, multi-match mailing company. Each package is hand-assembled and looks like its one-of-a-kind. RST even has a room full of mostly women hand-writing the addresses that go on the carrier envelope.

Others are putting the contents in FedEx and USPS Priority Mail envelopes. Others are affixing handwritten Post-it notes in strategic locations in the mailing. These are the kinds of packages you want to mail if you are trying to reach a corporate executive or if you are selling a high-end product or service.

RST also has laser printers that can print handwriting fonts in blue, thus looking nearly indistinguishable from true handwriting. If you want your letter to look like a truly personal letter (not mass-produced), RST is the shop for this.

Traditional high-volume direct mail.

The two vendors that do the most high-volume mailing are Veritis and MailAmerica (awful website, but they do great direct mail work, mailing about 200,000,000 letters a year). MailAmerica is superb for standard envelope packages (#10s, 9"x12"s. and other standard envelopes).

Veritis is an enormous company that can produce just about every format imaginable. Veritis is best known for its in-line self-mailers -- where the entire package is printed on one sheet of paper, then sliced,

148

folded up- and glued all kinds of ways. What this allows for is extensive personalization at low cost . . . and odd shaped packages that stand out in the mailbox. The catch?

Because of high set-up costs required by the big machines nearly the size of a football field, Veritis products are generally most cost-effective in very high-volumes (i.e. 500,000 pieces and up).

However, Veritis has now introduced a low-volume product designed for small business people. This is a template product, complete with graphic design. You just upload your text, and presto, your mailing can go out in a few days.

The minimum run for this product is 5,000 letters (which is a tiny mailing by direct marketing standards). Verities can also help you with copy writing, graphic art and data mining. It's a terrific company.

Database management.

Your list of hot prospects and satisfied customers is your business's most valuable asset. No matter what business you are in, you need a database to store names and keeps records of transactions.

You need to keep track of what people buy, how much they paid, and the dates of transactions. And, of course, you need their contact information. You need this information for many reasons, but one of the most important reasons is so that you can keep track of your "repeat buyers." One of the most important concepts in marketing is "recency" and "frequency."

You want to focus special attention on your "recent" buyers and "frequent" buyers. This is the lynch pin of capitalizing on the all-important 80/20 rule in marketing: 80 percent of your net income will come from 20 percent of your customers. These are your "recent" and "frequent" buyers. This is how you mine the gold from your customer list.

To do this you need a good database management system. You can either design your own in-house system. If you have a large mass-mailing program, you will want to hire a professional database management company to enter data, maintain, and manage your list of customers and leads.

There are many firms that can do this for you. Here are a few:

www.kayesmith.com,

www.merkleinc.com,

www.saturncorp.com,

www.data-management.com

I recommend you learn more about automating your systems (especially marketing and sales). The practice can kick your company to the next level of profitability. It will rapidly increase your income as well as save you time and money.

How To Publish Your Book Profitably

Writing, publishing and distributing your own book is one of the most powerful marketing strategies there is -- especially if you are a consultant, a doctor, a financial advisor, a lawyer, a Realtor, a teacher, or in a profession that requires specialized expertise (which is almost every profession).

There are few better credentials than having a book you've written in print. The cost to print a book is about the same as a four-color corporate brochure, but has 1,000 times more impact on your potential client.

If you're looking for a great way to establish your credentials, you can be a published author in your profession. People can refer to your book when they talk to their friends.

Books can be a great way to get your name in front of a preferred client or prospect. They might ignore your business card, but chances are they won't toss your book.

Few people outside of the book industry are aware of the amount of planning and work that goes into creating a finished book. If you don't have experience in this area you are probably going to have to enlist the expertise of a several professionals, or be willing to dedicate the time necessary to properly prepare yourself for the project.

You will need to learn about book design -- interior and exterior -- typography, editing, proof-reading, securing printer's quotes, how to obtain ISBN and CIP information, how to obtain an EAN and bar code, and why it is required, and how to distribute your books once they come back from the printer.

Make a few decisions about some very basic things, such as the book's, physical size and format, the type of paper you want the book being printed on, the art for the cover, and what kind of budget you'll have.

Good companies for short run books (fewer than 300 copies) are www.Lulu.com, www.infinitypublishing.com and www.OutskirtsPress.com. For best pricing and quality on longer runs, try Signature Books in Maryland. Another great company is Brenner printing; www.brennerprinting.com and for quality short-run printing of your book, go to www.morrispublishing.com.

Amazon.com has fully committed to the print on demand process with its website www.createspace.com. You can now produce an e-book and self-publish directly through Amazon.

Get your book on Amazon without going to the printer. Booksurge is a print-on-demand company that partners with Amazon.com to produce your books as needed. If you want to use another company, many of the print on demand companies will be able to get your book registered on Amazon.com as well.

Amazon now has its own POD service called CreateSpace. It's a one stop shop for print on demand.

The two biggest wholesale book distributors are Baker and Taylor and Ingram Publisher Services.

They will carry just about any book if you present it to them. Once your book is carried there, Amazon and Barnes & Noble have it. It's up to you to use the marketing know-how you are learning here to build a prairie fire of demand for your book. Distribution was once a problem for authors. Not anymore.

Other second-tier book (but good) distributors include. . .

Associated Publishers Group, Atlas Books, Bella Distribution, Book Clearing House, Fitzhenry & Whiteside, Consortium Book Sales, Cardinal Publishers Group, C&B Books Distribution, Greenleaf Book Group, Independent Publishers Group, Midpoint Trade Books, National Book Network, Small Press Distribution.

Some of these distributors specialize in certain kinds of books. Check out the links above to go to their websites and see which distributors are right for your book. To have your book distributed in stores and carried in libraries, you will need to get an ISBN number for each book you write.

ISBN stands for International Standard Book Number. You do that by going here: www.ISBN.org Your ISBN number appears as a barcode on the back on your book. You should also get a Library of Congress Number, also called a Cataloging in Publication Number.

This number along with a classification(s) description of the book appears on the copyright page. This further helps libraries and book dealers catalogue and categorize books. You can get this by going here: http://www.loc.gov/aba/

It's not very difficult to create and publish a book anymore. Contact me at www.DiDPublishng.com if you want to create your own book. We can help you write, edit and produce your book as well as market and distribute it for you.

The best part is you'll be able to have a marketable book to give to prospects and clients or you can sell them.

Useful Tools And Services

Telecasts and Conference Call Seminars

To talk to up to 2,000 people at the same time for $47 a month as often as you want, use www.Instantteleseminar.com as just a conventional conference call bridge line. Stop making one-on-one sales calls. Talk to hundreds, even thousands, of prospects and customers at the same time by holding a conference call seminar or telecast.

Here's a great way to record phone interviews with www.HotRecorder.com. This is great material for your website. It works for Internet-based phone services such as www.Skype.com.

I pay around $52.00 for the year for my Skype connection and that's pretty much it. The reception is pretty good and except for a few drops now and then; I'm satisfied.

You should be using an Internet based phone service. The benefits are numerous and because it's incredibly inexpensive, you can use it for home or office.

Pamela for Skype offers a great way to create podcasts and record phone interviews and conversations. This plug-in for Skype is the perfect tool for audio web blogs.

Affiliate program management and tracking

Options to look at include affordable hosted third-party solutions such as www.MyAffiliateProgram.com, www.AffiliateTracking.com, www.DirectTrack.com, and www.AffiliateShop.com.

If you want to install the software yourself and run it on your own server (thus avoiding monthly fees), www.AffiliateGuerilla.com and www.Groundbreak.com are good bets. www1ShoppingCart.com (the shopping cart I use) includes affiliate tracking in its bundle of eMerchant services -- valuable because, then you don't need to worry about integrating your affiliate program with your shopping cart.

If you're a big company looking to use the services of a full-fledged affiliate marketing service, other big corporations love to use www.ComissionJunction.com, www.BeFree.com and www.LinkShare.com (their fees are steep).

Website Hosting and Domain Names

The hosting service that I use is www.GoDaddy.com and www.HostGator.com. Another popular option is www.HostMonster.com. Some say HostMonster gives you more server space for your money. But I've been happy enough with HostGator and GoDaddy. Many of my associates use GoDaddy for domain purchasing.

Submit your site to search engines

Don't pay a company to do this. You can do this yourself in about three minutes. To add your site to Google, go to http://www.google.com/addurl/. To add your site to Yahoo, go to https://siteexplorer.search.yahoo.com/submit.

About 90 percent of searches are conducted using Google or Yahoo or by search engines that are powered by Google or Yahoo. But it's just as easy to submit your site to the other search engines as well.

Other search engines to submit your site to include: Inktomi, MSN, Ask.com, Open Directory Project, AltaVista, HotBot. Pay-Per-Click Advertising on Google, Yahoo and the Search Engines

Google AdWords is the #1 pay-per-click program on the Internet. Go here to get started: https://adwords.google.com/select/starter/signup/ForkAuth

Yahoo Search Marketing (formerly Overture) is the #2 pay-per-click advertising program. I use that with great success as well. But there are not nearly as many searches on Yahoo as Google. So it's tough to generate really big traffic with Yahoo but it's still very good.

Microsoft's pay per click program is not worth investigating yet, in my opinion. Go to https://adcenter.microsoft.com/ to try Microsoft's AdCenter program.

All the search engines have pay-per-click advertising programs. So do the Super Pages, the Yellow Pages and many of the big directories. PPC advertising is powerful and highly cost-effective because only those actually looking for your ad find your ad. And you pay only when someone actually clicks on your ad -- meaning you only pay for those who are actually interested in hearing what you have to say.

You aren't paying to reach people who have no interest in what you are saying or selling. In other words, this is target marketing to the nth degree.

Find your ideal niche on the web by tracking keywords . . . and your competition

Searches on the Internet are performed by people typing keywords and phrases into the search engine. You need to have the right keywords and phrases connected with your site if you are to rank high on the listings for the product you are selling or the theme of your site.

Website content that is closely tied to the keywords and phrases you've chosen and that your target market is typing into their search engines (to find what you are selling) is the foundation of your entire Internet marketing strategy.

This is critical for both your pay-per-click ad campaigns and for optimizing your site so that it achieves high rankings in the free (organic) search engine listings. Correct keyword selection for your site is really the lynchpin for building a profitable online business.

Yahoo's keyword selector tool is here: http://inventory.overture.com/d/searchinventory/suggestion/

Google's keyword research tool is here: https://adwords.google.com/select/KeywordToolExternal.

Google will also suggest keywords and phrases here for you to try if you type your URL here: https://adwords.google.com/select/KeywordToolExternal. This will help you select better keywords and phrases. . . as well as help you narrow the focus of your site or page (if too broad a range of keywords comes up in Google's list).

An excellent free keyword research tool can be found at www.GoodKeyWords.com.

I use this one quite often. www.WordTracker.com and www.KeyWordDiscovery.com are extremely good subscription keyword research and tracking services that allow you to drill deeper and go beyond what Google and Yahoo's free services allow you to do. But I think www.GoodKeyWords.com is easier to use; it's almost as good, plus, it's free.

Find how your site compares to your competition by going to Alexa, which you'll find at http://www.alexa.com/search. You can find how where your site ranks by just typing your URL into the search field.

There are more than 56 MILLION websites as of this writing. So if your site ranks in the top 560,000, that puts you in the top 1% of sites. But that's not all that important (unless you are trying to be a broad-based media property like Yahoo).

What is important is how you compare to your competitors. You can check their rankings on Alexa as well. Alexa will also reveal links pointing to the site and even show visitor reviews -- all saving you untold hours of market research.

But remember, all these are just tools that assist you. Don't follow their suggestions blindly. A power saw is a great tool. But human skill is required to make it effective. And poor use of it can be disastrous.

Product fulfillment

Go to the Mailing & Fulfillment Service Association's website at www.mfsanet.org to find a company in your local area suited to the number or units you are shipping every week. One of the biggest fulfillment operations is National Fulfillment Services. If you ship 50 units a week, that will require a different fulfillment operation. A small mom-and-pop shop in your local area will serve you best.

Order-Taking Call Centers

I have had very good success with In Service America at www.inserviceamerica.com, located not too far from me in Forest, Virginia. They can also handle fulfillment for your program. The big order taking phone center is West Teleservices at www.West.com which employs 29,000 people.

All the big-time direct marketers use them, but it's probably not suitable for small operations (high set-up charges) -- though they are very low cost if your volume of business is high. Otherwise In Service America will be better for you. Another even lower cost service is LiveOps at www.liveops.com They employ operators at home, which allows LiveOps to keep its overhead low and, therefore, its cost to you low.

If you want your call center to actually close sales for you (not just take orders), that costs substantially more. The leading call center sale closers are InPulse, Protocol Marketing and Triton Technology. These services provide script writers, database management and sophisticated tracking.

These are world-class marketers. You just sit back and watch them work their magic. Triton is paid by commission. So this eliminates your risk; but they also don't take just any project that comes along. These are the kinds of classic "Boiler Room" operations you see portrayed negatively (sometimes for good reason) by "60 Minutes." But they can be highly effective.

Ad and media buying agencies

There's a reason successful corporations hire ad and media buying agencies. They are worth it. The money they save you by knowing their business more than pays for their fees. They know how to negotiate the best deal and what media will bring back the best return on your investment (ROI).

Manhattan Media and Novus Media (good for your print ads). Mercury Media (TV ads). Mercury is a big direct response agency specializing in TV, but can also handle your radio and print ads. RevShare (TV ads) can be a great option because you pay based on

159

orders that come in. So you, RevShare and the TV station each take a share of the profits.

This difficulty is that not many TV stations will accept this arrangement. But it can be a great way to test a TV ad for low or zero risk. Radio Direct Response (radio ads) is a leader in direct response radio ads. Marketing Architects (radio) is another leader in direct response radio advertising (a bit on the pricey side, but very good). Tony Robbins and Carlton Sheets (huge direct sellers) are among MA's stable of high-profile clients.

DVD/CD duplication and packaging

A great company for this is SF Video. In quantities of 1,000 copies or more you can duplicate a CD for about 50 cents ea. and a DVD for about 75 cents ea.

They can also package CD and DVD sets for you in attractive cases for selling and ship them to your customers. Great if you are in the seminar business . . . or if you are selling or mass-producing any kind of digital media.

How to look bigger than you really are

Within about five minutes, www.Angel.com will allow you to have a world-class customer service call center that will make you sound like a Fortune 500 Company.

Here's a company that, starting at $9.99 per month), provides call screening, toll-free numbers, fax service, voicemail, extensions with menu prompts and more; they're called www.RingCentral.com.

If you need a physical office sometimes, but not most of the time, take a look at www.OfficeSuitesPlus.com, www.OfficeGeneral.com, or www.HQ.com.

These services will provide office space on demand, complete with conference rooms, Internet connections, receptionist, support staff, phones, copiers, fax machines, computers and all the gadgets and gizmos you'd want in an office -- even a panoramic 20th floor view of the city you're in.

Why pay for office space when you aren't using it? And why have an office only in one place?

Instead, have an office wherever you happen to be. Not only does this modus operandi make you look big, it allows you total mobility and freedom.

Find a Celebrity to Endorse Your Product

Finding the right celebrity to endorse your product can often increase response to your marketing by 100% or more. Most cost-effective is to have a well-respected celebrity who is semi-retired. For example, we were able to get a member of "The Partridge Family" to endorse a product of a client of mine for a few thousand dollars, and it's made the difference between stunning success and failure for the campaign.

Very often you can sign for an entire year celebrities (movie stars, Hall-of-Fame athletes, etc.) who are not current box office superstars, but were at one time and are still very well-known and respected, for $20,000. Good celebrity brokers include Celeb Brokers and Celebrity Endorsement Network.

And often you can just do-it-yourself by using a directory called Contact Any Celebrity.

If just 2% of the 1,000 celebrities you write, send back the authorization form giving you permission to list the celebrity as a "Friend of [Org Name]" on the letterhead and website, you then have a list of 20 celebrities you can list as friends (with photos) in direct mail solicitations, on the website and other promotional material. This will usually increase response to your mailing 50%-100% or even more.

The key to success here is to pick celebrities (usually older celebrities) who people respect and admire. Michael Jackson, Mike Tyson and Michael Vick (the three "Michaels") are well-known, but would not be good choices. But baseball great Cal Ripkin would be good for many products because of his wholesome all-American image.

You also want the celebrity endorser to fit the product -- i.e. Kirstie Alley's endorsement of the Jenny Craig weight-loss program (assuming she does not balloon out again). The endorsement needs to make sense.

Product Design, Development and Distribution

Are you an inventor? Do you have an idea for a product? Looking for a partner to help you develop the prototype, build it, market it and distribute it globally? Then BJ Global Direct might be your ticket.

BJ Global is an integrated design, manufacturing, marketing, and distribution company specializing in developing direct response and retail products for consumers. They have developed a formula for success.

Special thanks to Ben Hart for many of the helpful tips and suggestions for this section. Check out his website www.marketingrocketfuel.com. He has a great resource website for people who are interested in furthering their knowledge of direct marketing.

Your Next Move

This book is a companion to my online Core Training Program. It was designed to allow busy people to quickly grasp the big picture and later access the areas they feel will help them to develop the details within a viable strategy for real revenue growth.

The program helps business owners to craft a viable strategy for real income growth. By focusing on their list of prospects and clients, they can develop relationships for their long-term success.

Last bit of advice:

Please don't try something for a month and back off because it "didn't pan out." It takes at least a full three months of consistent effort to evaluate a program.

Short term thinking only leads to short term profits. The website www.doublemyrevenues.com is available for your further education. There are articles available for developing your plan.

There are articles geared toward doubling your income. There are interviews with experts in business and technology who will help you continue to refine your plans and procedures.

As a small business consultant and a business owner, I'll tell you that going through it alone is tough. There is no need to go through it alone anymore. Let the collective knowledge of a group of fellow business owners help you to succeed consistently. We work together to assure our mutual growth. Subscribe to my DMR updates; it's free.

Go to www.doublemyrevenues.com and sign up for your free updates.

Each month, we give you content that is geared toward one thing; to double your revenues. Stick with us and we'll help you to grow prosperous in your chosen venture. There are other courses offered in specific areas dealing with the topics we've covered. We'll highlight the best of them and steer you clear of the time-wasters.

You'll get regular coaching, seminars and interviews, tools and templates added to the library each month. You'll get reviews of programs and applications that help small businesses to grow their sales.

If you don't succeed even with our help, you'll get your money back. We have a 30 day money back guarantee but I'm so confident that you can make a difference, that I'll extend this offer to you right now. Good luck on your goals and remember that I can be reached by email dennis@didpublishing.com or by phone at 209-200-9562.

About the Author

Dennis Morales Francis is a small business coach and publications consultant based in Northern California. His experience in advertising and marketing goes back to the 1980's.

He has worked in a variety of media; the Internet, newspaper, Yellow pages, magazines, television, movies and even comics.

"I've published fiction and non-fiction books on a variety of subjects and have written hundreds of articles. I work with my clients personally to help them get their content to its intended target."

Dennis currently coaches small businesses in advertising and marketing on and off the Web. He teaches business owners the strategies for developing automatic marketing using articles, video, audiobooks and blogging. As a publications consultant, he produces designs and promotes books and manuals for other small business owners.

Dennis is the author of Push Button Profits, How to Make $120,000 a Year on Autopilot"

Go to DiD Publishing.com for more information on publications design and marketing.

The Internet Glossary

The good folks at Names@Work created a very good glossary of terms for Internet marketing and Web related words. I include it here for those that are still struggling with the medium. There are more exciting developments coming on the Internet that will simply amaze you; enjoy the ride. Check these folks for great information and rock solid Internet marketing support.

Go to http://www.namesatwork.com.

This partial list gives you a sense of what they do:

* Put together a winning business plan

* Identify new revenue opportunities (there are many)

* Raise money from knowledgeable investors

* Complete the ICANN application

* Publish policies that work for your TLD

* Find and engage a reliable registry operator

* Find and engage a reliable auction provider

* Plan and publicize the Sunrise Period to trademark holders

* Engage your community and get public support

* Secure political backing when required

* Deal with competition and contention

Glossary of Internet Marketing Terms

A

Above the Fold

The top portion of a web document that can be viewed without scrolling down.

AdSense

Google's contextual ad program for website publishers. Publishers place text ads provided by Google on their site, and earn a portion of the click through revenue.

Adwords

Google's contextual ad program for advertisers. Advertisers receive preferred placement (as Sponsored Links) for given keywords, based on a pay-per-click revenue model.

Related Definitions - Adsense Google

Affiliate Link

Links between a main company website and affiliate sites (sites selling products from main site or with referral links to main site). Affiliate linking contributes to Link Popularity, and is often used to generate traffic from niche markets.

Related Definitions - Link Popularity, Niche Market, Aggregation (See: RSS Aggregation)

Algorithm

The detailed sequence of actions used by search engines to rank web pages. The most famous Search Engine Algorithm is PageRank – Google's indexing method that assigns different weights to multiple variables of a website, including: keyword density, link popularity, website authority, etc. See: PageRank

Related Definitions - Authority, Google, Keyword, Density, Link Popularity,   PageRank, Search Engine,

AltaVista

One of the first major search engines, Later acquired by Overture.

See: www.altavista.com.

Related Definitions - Overture, Search Engine

Alternative Text (ALT Text)

The text placed inside graphic image tags in HTML code. The ALT text will show if an image fails to download, or for text-only browsers and screen readers.

ALT Tag: The tag defining the image text, found in the image tag

Related Definitions - Keyword, HTML, Screen Reader, Anchor Text (See: Link Text)

Ask.com

This is a very popular metasearch engine based on Question/Answer queries and results rather than direct search term queries. For more information, see: www.ask.com

Related Definitions - Search Engine

ASP (Active Server Page)

A scripting language developed by Microsoft to create websites with dynamic content.

Authority

For search engines, Authority is a measure of the number of links (or citations) pointing to a given site. In this sense, highly authoritative sites are those that have high link popularity (the internet method of peer-review).

Related Links - Link Popularity, PageRank

B

Backlink

Beta

The final testing phase for a software product before final release –is usually available online, but as an unfinished product.

Bid

The amount an advertiser is willing to pay for AdWords traffic per click.

Related Definitions - AdWords, Pay Per Click, Traffic,

Black Hat SEO

Optimization methods that intentionally break the rules set by search engines to trick the page rank algorithm. Black Hat SEO techniques negatively affect the viewer experience because they use spam to return less relevant results. Evidence of Black Hat SEO is grounds for exclusion from a search engine index or directory listing.

Blog

(Weblog)

A frequently updated website involving reverse-chronological "posts" –or, short opinion, news, or gossip updates, with a collaborative interface. Though blogs originated as a form of live journal, today they are a form of real-time publication media for individual web users. Since 2004, blogs have gained increasing credibility as an influential source of news, political power, and consumer trends.

Business Blog: Blog run by a corporate representative (or group of representatives) to discuss topics related to the company. Business blogs may be used for customer relations, brand reputation management, brand development, or search engine optimization. For more information, see: www.namesatwork.com/blogs

For more information on business blogging for Fortune 500 companies, see: www.socialtext.net

Related Definitions - Blog Carnival, Post

Blog Carnival

A topical collection of blog posts hosted by a rotating list of participating blogs. Participants contribute a post of their choice each week, to be reviewed and linked to by the carnival host. In turn, participants link to the host site as publicity for the carnival. Blog carnivals are a means of pooling traffic from participating sites, to take advantage of the aggregate popularity of a set of blogs.

For more information about blog carnivals, see www.blogcarnival.com

Related Definitions - Blog, Blogroll

Blogroll

A collection of links to other blogs, usually found in the sidebar.

Related Definitions - Blog, Blog Carnival

Body Text

The visible text on a webpage between the "and" tags in HTML code. Types of body text include text inside headings, paragraphs, lists and tables.

Boolean Search

A search method using operators such as AND, OR, and NOT to refine a search.

Brand Value

The intangible value associated with brand awareness, image, reputation, and loyalty.

Broken Link

A link that doesn't work or doesn't lead anywhere, usually appearing as a 404 Error.

Browser

A program that translates coded pages (in HTML, Javascript, etc.), allowing users to users to navigate the Internet.

Buzz Marketing

Type of Word of Mouth Marketing that attracts consumer and media attention by generating entertaining, conversation-worthy 'buzz' around a brand.

Double My Revenues In 12 Months Or Less

Related Definitions - Buzzword

Buzzword

A popular trend word.

C

CGI (Common Gateway Interface)

A server-side communication interface that enables data exchange between HTML pages and external programs.

Related Definitions - HTML

Click Stream

The recorded click path of an Internet visitor through one or more website links.

Related Definitions - Click Through

CTR

Click Through

Action taken by a visitor to click on an advertising link and arrive at an indexed site.

Click Through Rate (CTR)

The ratio between the number of clicks on an ad and the number of page impressions delivered to the ad arrival site.

Related Definitions - Click Stream, Pay Per Click

Cloaking

The process of masking keyword-heavy content in the hidden text of a webpage. Cloaking is a black-hat SEO technique, and is grounds for de-listing from a search engine or directory.

Related Definitions - Black-Hat SEO, De-Listing, Search Engine

Comment

1. HTML tags used to insert explanations of code that won't be visible to users. Comments tags are largely ignored because they were at one point abused by keyword-spammers. Comments are placed between < !- - comments - - >

2. Blog reader's reply to a specific post. Comments allow for interactive participation from viewers, and often serve as discussion spaces on a blog.

Compatibility

The ability of a website to be integrated into (or read by) different web browsers. Website compatibility is generally associated with complying with W3C standards. For more information, see: www.w3.org

Double My Revenues In 12 Months Or Less

Related Definitions - Browser Usability

Competitive Analysis

Assessment of the strengths and weaknesses of a business as compared to its competitors.

Related Definitions - Gap Analysis

Consumer Generated Media (CGM)

Media based on consumer-to-consumer information sharing networks. Types of Consumer Generated Media include blogs, forums, discussion boards, Flickr, MySpace, and other social networking software.

For more information, see: FC Now

Related Definitions - Blog, Podcast, RSS, Vlog

Content Management

The acquisition, organization, and publication of digital content on the Internet.

Content Management System (CMS): System developed to manage the acquisition, organization and publication of digital content on the Internet.

Related Definitions - Compatibility, Usability

175

Contextual Advertising

Displaying ads that match the nearby text on a web page. For example, if a user is viewing a website about downloading music, the ads displayed might be in a music program like iTunes or Limewire.

Related Definitions - Adsense, Adwords

Conversion

A website visitor completing a desired action. Types of conversions include signing up for a newsletter, buying a product or service, registering to receive more information, joining an email list, and other transactions.

Related Definitions - Conversion Point, Conversion Rate

Conversion Point

The point at which a visitor has completed desired action – usually denoted by a "thank you" page, or a return to the homepage.

Related Definitions - Conversion, Conversion Rate

Conversion Rate

A measure of the number of visitors who follow a call to action on a website. Calls to action include: purchasing goods or services, subscribing to a newsletter or email list, contacting the website provider, entering personal information, etc.

Related Definitions - Click-through, Conversion, Conversion Point, Visitor

Cost-Per-Click (CPC)

Amount paid for each click-through from an ad to the advertiser's website.

Related Definitions - AdSense, AdWords, Bid, Pay-Per-Click

Crawler

See: Spider

Crawler Lag

The delay between the point when a web page is scanned by a crawler (or spider) and the point at which it is added to the search engine database.

Related Definitions - Database, Search Engine, and Spider

Cross Linking

Linking between related websites – either related by owner, as business affiliates, or within the same niche community. Cross-linking is used as a way to build link popularity, and in excess is considered a form of spam.

Related Definitions - Affiliate Links, Link Popularity, Link Building, Black-Hat SEO

CSS (Cascading Style Sheets)

Website format used to define the style elements of an HTML document.

Related Definitions - HTML

Customer Relations Management (CRM)

The management of relationships with potential and current customers to better meet customer needs and identify business development opportunities.

Cyber squatting

The practice of registering an unused domain name for the purpose of selling it back at an inflated price. This is usually done with trademarked or branded domain names, or names very similar to a trademark or brand.

D

Database

A collection of information. For search engines, the storage body for information gathered by the search engine spider, organized by the index, and held for retrieval by the user interface.

Related Definitions - Index, Search Engine, Spider

Dead Link

See: Broken Link

Deep Linking

Linking to pages embedded in a website's hierarchy, rather than to entrance pages.

De-Listing

The removal of a website from a search engine or directory index–usually for breaking the search engine or directory rules.

Related Definitions - Black Hat SEO, Spam

Directory

An internet index categorized by human editors – as opposed to a search engine, which is categorized according to automatic algorithms.

DogPile

A metasearch engine. For more information, see: www.dogpile.com

Domain Name

A unique name corresponding to an IP Address.

Ex: www.namesatwork.com

Domain Name Portfolio

A collection of domain names

Domain Name Tasting

Testing and monetizing a domain name during the 5-day grace period after purchase that allows a return and full refund.

For more information on Domain Tasting, visit: ICANN Wiki

Doorway Page

See: Landing Page

Dynamic Content

Content that changes automatically in response to user input, or at regular intervals.

E

Entry Page

See: Landing Page

Exact Match

Search query in quotation marks, used to find an exact phrase or key term.

Excite

A popular search engine. For more information, visit: Excite

External Links

Links to and from one website and another. The quantity and quality of external links related to a website affect the website's overall Page Rank.

Inbound Link: Link pointing towards a website.

Outbound Link: Link pointing out of a website.

Related Definitions: Internal Links, Page Rank, Link Popularity, and Link Building.

Evangelist

An emotive individual who voluntarily markets a trend to recruit new followers.

Customer Evangelist: A loyal customer who adamantly promotes a brand, and acts as a powerful word of mouth marketing vehicle.

Related Definitions - Influencer, Word of Mouth Marketing, Ezine

Online magazine publication –typically delivered via email.

F

Facebook

Facebook is a social media service that was released in February of 2004. The social media website has over 845 million active customers worldwide. The members known as "friends" must first register before using website; they can then produce a personal profile, add other "friends" to their network, and exchange messages, including automatic notices once they update their profile.

Feed

See: RSS Feed

Feed Reader

See: RSS Feed Reader

Flash

Software originally developed by Macromedia (currently owned by Adobe) used to create animated graphics for websites, games, and other desktop presentations.

Flickr

A website developed by Ludicorp as a digital photo sharing service. Flickr is an example of User Generated Content.

Related Definitions - User Generated Content

Footprint

The elements of a web page that affect search engine ranking but are not located on the page itself.

Forum

An open online discussion space for individuals who share a niche interest.

Related Definitions - Blog, RSS, User Generated Content

Frames

HTML construct that allows two or more HTML documents to be displayed in a single web browser screen as separately scrollable regions.

Full-Text Search

The ability to search the entire contents of a digital document.

G

Gap Analysis

An assessment of the variance between the actual (current) performance and the potential performance of a business system.

Ghost Site

A website that is no longer maintained but is still available online.

Google

Currently the most popular search engine, with the largest database and arguably the most accurate search results. Google pioneered the PageRank algorithm as a means of indexing websites and other web documents. For more information about Google services, see: Google.

Google Maps

Google Maps is a web mapping service application and technology provided by Google, that powers many map-based services, including the Google Maps website,

H

Header

The top region of a website that contains the page title and URL.

Heading

An HTML tag that assigns greater weight to a set of keywords. The excessive use of headers to increase keyword strength for SEO can be grounds for de-listing.

Related Definitions - De-listing, SEO

Hidden Text

Text that is visible only to search engines, usually for the purpose of artificially inflating keyword density. Keyword spamming through hidden text is grounds for de-listing from a search engine.

Related Definitions - De-listing, Keyword Density, Search Engine

Hit

A single file request from a web server. Note: There may be many hits for a single page view. Hits are a preliminary measure of website activity, but are a poor measure of the number of visitors.

Related Definitions - Impression, Traffic, Unique Visitor, Visitor

Home Page

The main point of entry for a website.

Related Definitions - Landing Page

Hyperlink Text

See: Link Text

HTML

Hypertext Markup Language: The publishing language of the Internet; a coding language used to create hypertext documents for the web.

Related Definitions - Hypertext

HTTP (Hyper Text Transfer Protocol)

The protocol that enables digital file transmission over the Internet.

Related Definitions - Domain Name,

Hub

An authoritative website that links to other sites related to a niche topic.

Related Definitions - Influencer, Page Rank

Hypertext

Text that is cross-linked to other documents.

Related Definitions - HTML, Hyperlink

I

Image Tag

Command to retrieve a given image file from a web server.

Related Definitions - HTML, URL

Image Map

A graphic containing two or more clickable hyperlinked regions.

Impression

A single display of an online advertisement. Banner advertisements are sometimes measured according to Cost Per (1000) Impressions (CPM).

Inbound Link

See: External Link

Index

Information organized in a search engine database.

Indexer: Tool that organizes information for the search engine database.

Indexing: Process of storing information as an ordered collection.

Related Definitions - Database, Search Engine, and Spider

Influencer

Influential individual who is recognized as an expert in a subject, and acts as a powerful word of mouth marketing vehicle.

Related Definitions - Blog, Evangelist, Word of Mouth Marketing

Intranet

A network of web documents that is only accessible to people within a specific group or organization. Like the Internet, an intranet is used to share information within an enterprise.

Intent Categories

The definition of a search term is in part informed by the searcher's intent.

Intent is divided into three different categories:

Informational: User is searching for information about a topic.

Navigational: User is searching for a specific web page or website.

Transactional: User is seeking to make a transaction online – to buy, rent, subscribe, download, or follow a call to action.

Related Definitions- Search Engine Optimization, Search Term

Internal Links

Links to and from pages within a website. The quantity and quality of internal links related to a page determines that page's importance in the overall website hierarchy.

Related Definitions - External Links, Link Popularity, Link Building

Invisible Text

See: Hidden Text

IP (Internet Protocol)

The standards that enable the transfer of data between dissimilar networks. IP and TCP (Transmission Control Protocol) are the essential components of the Internet.

Related Definitions - IP Address

IP Address

The numeric identification code assigned to every user and every server online.

Related Definitions - TCP

J

Java

A cross-platform programming language originally developed by Sun Microsystems, used to create complex programs that can run on multiple different operating systems, for easy Internet distribution.

K

Keyword

A significant word used as a reference point to find more information.

Related Definitions - Title Tag, Meta Tags, Alternative Text, Hyperlink Text, Body Text, Search Term, Keyword Density

Keyword Density

The ratio of the number of times a keyword appears within a web page's text.

Keyword Relevance

A measure of the relevance of a website to a keyword (or set of keywords) used in a search query. Keyword Relevance is primarily measured by the use of keywords in the title tag, meta tags, alternative text, hyperlink text, or document text of a website.

Keyword Research

See: Search Term Research

L

Landing Page

The page a visitor arrives at after clicking a link (from an advertisement, search engine results page, email, or other type of hyperlink). Also called an Entry Page.

Related Definitions - Home Page, Link, Visitor

Link

1. An image or segment of text that serves as a cross reference between parts of a website or web document.

2. In HTML: A specific URL between the < .a href> and tags.

Related Definitions - External Links, Hyperlink Text, Internal Links, Link Building, Link Popularity

LinkedIn

LinkedIn is a business-related social networking site that was launched in May 2003. The social networking site is mainly used for professional networking. As of 9 February 2012, LinkedIn reports more than 150 million registered users in more than 200 countries and territories.

Link Building

The process of researching, requesting, and creating inbound links to a website, to increase link popularity.

Related Definitions - Link Popularity, Inbound Links, Page Rank

Link Farm

A page used to boost link popularity by allowing users to register their website and receive an inbound link. Being associated with link farms decreases a site's search engine rankings.

Link Popularity

A measure of the quantity and quality of internal and external links associated with a website.

Related Definitions - Internal Links, External Links, Link Building

Link PR

The distribution of link-embedded press release content to multiple RSS news aggregators. Link PR, also called Search, PR, is a means of spreading inbound links by incorporating them into newsworthy RSS content that can be re-distributed by other news sites.

Link Text

The text contained within a link.

Related Definitions - External Links, Hyperlink, Hyperlink Text, Internal Links, Link Building, Link Popularity

Log File

File stored by the server of each website that records traffic statistics, including: visitors, unique visitors, visitor IP address, page views, hits, etc. Analysis of the log file is essential to measuring the progress of SEO and the usability of a website.

The Long Tail

The economic concept first coined by Chris Anderson in 2004 to describe the distribution of wealth on the Internet. The Long Tail represents the millions of niche market audiences that drive the majority of sales for sites such as Amazon and EBay.

Related Definitions - Niche Market

M

Meta Search

Type of search performed across multiple search engines – on a meta search engine.

Meta Tag

An HTML tag that gives information about the content of a website. Meta tags are non-visible text, that helps define your website for search engine spiders.

Related Definitions - Spider, HTML

Micro-Site

A small, closely linked network of related web pages within a larger website.

Mozilla Firefox

A popular open-source, cross-platform browser, developed by the Mozilla Foundation.

Myspace

Myspace is a social networking service launched in August 2003 and hosts over 33.1 million unique U.S. visitors.

N

Natural Language Processing

The intelligent translation of natural language phrases into keyword search queries. Natural Language Processing programs use multi-level linguistic statistics and analysis to "understand" human language queries.

Natural Link

A hyperlink included in natural language text for the purpose of expanding an idea, and not necessarily with the intention of increasing link popularity.

Related Definitions - Link, Link Popularity, Natural Language Processing, Natural Traffic

Natural Traffic

Traffic from directly typed-in domain names or URLs.

Related Definitions - Domain Name, Natural Link

Newsgroup

See: Forum

Niche Market

A specifically-focused market segment. Niche Markets are often discussed in the context of the Long Tail – or the economic concept that the distribution of wealth on the Internet is a "long tail" made up of millions of niche markets.

Related Definitions - Long Tail, Word of Mouth Marketing

No Follow Tag

A tag that directs search engines to skip certain pages: rel="nofollow"

O

Off Page

See: Footprint

Operators

Boolean search words that inform search results, but are not considered keywords: AND, OR, NOT

Related Definitions - Boolean Search

Optimization

The process of improving a website for search engine visibility. Optimization may include building keyword density, link popularity, search engine compatibility, and/or improving layout/design.

Outbound Link

See: External Link

Overture

A search engine that returns results based on paid placement rather than algorithmic rankings. Overture is currently owned by Yahoo!

P

Page Impression

See: Impression

Page Rank

The algorithm used to determine the hierarchy of pages and websites in the search engine index. Devised by Google, Page Rank is a measure of the quality and quantity of traffic, links, visitors, and keyword content of a website.

Although the Page Rank algorithm is kept secret by Google, it is widely discussed by search engine optimization experts. For more information about the factors that affect page rank, see: www.seomoz.org

Related Definitions - Google, Keyword, Link, Search Engine Optimization, Visitors

Page View

Single request to load a full HTML page (as opposed to Hits – single requests to load each file in an HTML page)

Related Definitions - Hit, HTML, Traffic

Paid Placement

A program that allows advertisers to pay for placement on the search results page.

Related Definitions - Search Results Page, PPC

Partial Match

Search results that match all or part of a keyword phrase.

Pay-Per-Click (PPC)

An advertising payment model that allows advertisers to bid on keywords and pay only when the ad is clicked, thus paying for actual traffic rather than page impressions. The highest keyword bidders receive the highest rankings in search engine results pages, and therefore, the most traffic. The PPC model was first introduced to search by Overture, and made famous by the enormous profits generated by Google's Adsense and Adwords programs.

Podcast

A digital audio file that is distributed through RSS feeds, usually at regular intervals as a radio broadcast.

Related Definitions - Blog, RSS, Vlog

Portal

A website that acts as a starting point for web users, usually offering browser services such as customized search, email, news updates, etc.

Related Definitions - Yahoo!

Positioning

The process of optimizing a website for a target audience.

Related Definitions - Optimization

Post

A time-stamped article published on a blog.

Related Definitions - Blog

PPC

See: Pay Per Click

Q

Query

A keyword phrase used to request information from a search engine.

R

Ranking

See: Page Rank

Reciprocal Link

Link exchange between two websites.

Related Definitions - Link, Link Popularity

Referrer

A webpage referring users to another page with a link.

Refresh

The button used to reload a web page. The refresh command can also be included as an HTML tag used to automatically redirect visitors to another page. This type of automatic redirection is considered spam, and is grounds for de-listing.

Relevance

A measure of how closely the search engine results match a search query – or, a measure of how closely search results match the information sought by the user. Arguably the most relevant search engine today, Google assesses the website relevance through its complex Page Rank algorithm.

Related Definitions - Google, Page Rank

Robot

An automatic program that scans websites by following links. See: Spider

Related Definitions - Search Engine, Spider

ROI (Return on Investment)

Percentage of profit returned for the funds invested to produce it. In terms of search engine optimization, ROI refers to the sales directly attributed to an SEO or SEM campaign.

RSS (Really Simple Syndication)

Digital content syndicated to a specified source (the RSS feed reader) as a convenient way to collect information quickly from multiple sources. Any digital content – text, images, audio files, or video files – can be streamed through RSS. RSS is most commonly used as a way to gather regularly updated content, such as blog posts, and podcasts or news headlines.

RSS Aggregation: the collection of RSS feeds

RSS Feed

The digital content syndicated through RSS readers.

RSS Feed Reader (or RSS Aggregator)

An information management program that gathers and translates RSS feeds.

RSS Subscription

To sign up for a specific RSS feed and have feed updates sent regularly to an email address, or RSS feed reader.

S

Screen Reader

A device for visually impaired users that translates the contents of a webpage into Braille or speech.

Search Engine

A tool for finding information on the Internet. Search engines use a complex Page Rank algorithm to categorize websites and web documents. The basic components of a search engine are:

1. Spiders /Crawlers- gather information

2. Indexer – categorizes information

3. Database – stores information

4. Search Engine Software – uses page rank algorithm to retrieve information from the index and return it to the website interface.

5. Website Interface – the website used by viewers to retrieve information related to a search query.

Related Definitions - Database, Page Rank, Search Engine Optimization, Search, Query, Spider

Search Engine Marketing

The process of marketing a website through search engines. Search engine marketing drives traffic by paying for ad words, page rank and/or inbound links.

Related Definitions - Pay Per Click, Paid Placement, Search Engine Optimization

Search Engine Optimization

The process of optimizing a website to improve search engine ranking. Search Engine Optimization is often divided into two different schools: White Hat SEO and Black Hat SEO

Search Engine Optimization differs from Search Engine Marketing, in that SEO involves only natural (unpaid) techniques to improve search engine ranking, and SEM involves paid ads or paid placement. Both SEO and SEM are used to increase website traffic, conversions, page rank, and ROI.

Related Definitions - Black Hat SEO, Conversions, Page Rank, Search Engine Marketing, White Hat SEO,

Search Engine Spider

See: Spider

Search Term (or Search Query)

Keyword phrase used to find information through a search engine. Search terms are defined both by the lexical meaning of a keyword and by the intent of the searcher. See: Intent Categories

Related Definitions - Intent Categories, Keyword, Search Engine

Search Term Research (STR)

Discovery and analysis of keywords (or word) to target for an SEO or SEM campaign.

Related Definitions - Keyword, Search Engine Marketing, Search Engine Optimization, Search Term

Search Query

See: Query

SEM

See: Search Engine Marketing

SEO

See: Search Engine Optimization

SERP (Search Engine Results Page)

The results listed by the search engine for a given search query. SERPs display listings in descending order of relevance to the search query.

SiteMap

paralink

A hierarchical list with links to all pages on a website. Used to show the structure of a site and aid navigation.

Social Bookmarking

The process of sharing a personal collection of bookmarks with a network of Internet users. "Bookmarks" may include favorite photos, websites, music, news articles, blog posts, or other online content. For more information, see del.icio.us

Related Definitions - Blog, Podcast, Post, RSS, Vlog

Spam

Double My Revenues In 12 Months Or Less

An unsolicited advertisement or Black Hat SEO tactic.

Related Definitions - Black Hat SEO, Search Engine Marketing, Search Engine Optimization

Spider (or Spyder)

A program that constantly scans the internet to collect information for search engines. Spiders follow internal and external links to create an index of all documents on the Internet.

Also called a "crawler".

Related Definitions - External Links, Internal Links, Search Engine

Splash Page

An image-based branding page shown before the home page (usually done in Macromedia Flash).

Related Definitions - Flash, Home Page

Sponsored Links

Paid placement advertisement links. Usually found at the top or on the sidebar of a search engine results page.

Submission

Submission of a web page title, description, and link to a search engine or directory, to be included in the index. Submissions may either be done automatically or manually.

Subscription

See: RSS Subscription.

T

Tagging

Labeling a blog post, image, or audio file with a set of keywords, for the purpose of categorization and recovery. Tagging is most often used for social bookmarking sites, blog directories, or user generated media.

Tag Cloud

A list of tag groups, displayed in "cloud" formation and in varying font sizes. A tag in larger font denotes a larger or more frequently visited group, whereas a smaller font denotes a smaller or less popular tag group.

Related Definitions - Blog, Flickr, Podcast, RSS, Social Bookmarking, Consumer Generated Media, Vlog

Target Site Analysis

Analysis of traffic patterns, keyword density, link popularity, and structure, for a specific website.

Related Definitions - Keyword, Keyword Density, Link Popularity

Traffic

TCP (Transmission Control Protocol)

The standards that enable one network to translate web data received from another dissimilar network. TCP and IP are the essential components of the Internet.

Related Definitions - IP

Teoma

A popular search engine that values subject-specific popularity over link popularity in its ranking algorithm. For more information, see: www.teoma.com

Related Definitions - Search Engine

Title Tag

An HTML tag defining the title of a page, as displayed at the top of the browser. The title is an important element used by search engines to determine a page's relevance to a given search query.

Related Definitions - HTML, Page Rank, Search Engine,

TLD (Top Level Domain)

The rightmost extension at the end of a domain name following the dot. Top Level Domains include both Generic Top Level Domains (gTLDs) and Country Code Top Level Domains (ccTLDs)

gTLDs: .com, .net, .org, .edu, .info, .biz, .gov, etc.

For more information, see: www.icann.org

ccTLDs: .uk, .fr, .au, .de, .es, .eu, etc.

For a full list, see: www.iana.org

Traffic

The number of files served or visitors to a website. Traffic may be measured by hits, impressions, clicks, page views, visitors, unique visitors, or other indications of website activity.

Related Definitions - Click-Through-Rate, Hit, Impression, Page view, Unique Visitor

Twitter

Twitter is an online social media service. The microblogging giant allows its customers to transmit and browse text-based posts in 140 characters. These posts are referred to as "tweets". Twitter was launched in March 2006 by Jack Dorsey. Over 140 million active customers produce over 340 million tweets daily and handling over 1.6 billion search queries daily.

U

Unique Visitor

An individual Internet user accessing a website over a period of time. The log file for a single unique visitor may show multiple visits, thus the importance of differentiating between "visitor" and "unique visitor" when measuring website statistics.

Related Definitions - Log File, Visitor

URL (Uniform Resource Locator)

The "address", or location, of a resource on the Internet.

Usability

The ease of user navigation and comprehension of a website.

User Generated Media

See: Consumer Generated Media

V

Viral Marketing

A marketing technique that takes advantage of pre-existing online networks to encourage the spread of advertising information by "word of mouth".

Related Definitions - Buzz Marketing, Evangelist, Influencer, Word of Mouth Marketing

Visibility (Website Visibility)

Measure of a website's ranking in search engines or directories.

Visitor

A single instance of an individual Internet user accessing a website. Not to be confused with a Unique Visitor.

Vlog (Video Blog)

A weblog that uses video content as its primary media - streaming video files through RSS like a podcast or blog feed.

Related Definitions - Blog, Podcast, RSS

W

Weblog

See: Blog

White Hat SEO

Ethical SEO methods that adhere to the rules set by search engines. White Hat SEO is concerned with improving page ranking and increasing traffic by naturally increasing the keyword relevance of a website.

Related Definitions - Black Hat SEO, Keyword Relevance, Page Rank, Search Engine

WHOIS

An Internet database providing information on the name server, registrar, and contact information for each domain name.

Related Definitions - Domain Name

Word of Mouth Marketing

A marketing technique that uses pre-existing social networks to spread publicity information by word of mouth.

Related Definitions - Buzz Marketing, Evangelist, Influencer, Link PR, Viral Marketing

X

XML (Extensible Markup Language)

A standard for creating markup languages that describe the structure of data. XML was developed by the W3C to create a common information format for data sharing between different systems.

Y

Yahoo!

A popular web portal and directory.

For more information, see: Yahoo!

Related Definitions - Directory, Portal

Z

Zone Search

An advanced search that limits results to a particular topic area (or zone).